FROM MAN TO GOD

FROM MAN TO GOD

An LDS Scientist Views Creation, Progression and Exaltation

WILLIAM E. HARRIS

Copyright © 1989
Horizon Publishers & Distributors, Inc.

All rights reserved. Reproduction in whole or any
parts thereof in any form or by any media without
written permission is prohibited.

ISBN: 0-88290-345-4
Library of Congress Catalog Card Number: 89-083433
Horizon Publishers' Catalog and Order Number: 1024
First Printing, March, 1989

Printing: 1 2 3 4 5 6 7 8 9 10

Printed and distributed
in the United States of America by

& Distributors, Incorporated
P.O. Box 490 Bountiful, Utah 84010-0490

Acknowledgement and Dedication

I wish to thank Hugh Rush, Michelle Barnson and Zina Reynolds, for their encouragement in the writing of this book.

This book is dedicated to my wife Minnie, to my children John, Bill, Nancy, David, and Jonathan, to my grandchildren, and to those who find joy in discovery.

TABLE OF CONTENTS

FORWARD 7

1. VIEWPOINTS 11
Two Points of View 11
Evolutionists 12
Matter, Space and Time 14
Creationists 17
Joseph Smith as a Scientist 18
Our Educational Limits 21
Speciation, One Form of Evolution 23

2. THE CREATION OF LIFE 26
The Origin of Species 26
Mutations 28
Evolutionary Jumps 30
Longevity of Man 32
Adam as a Creator 33
Pre-Historic Man 35
The Final Quarter of the Senior Year 37

3. BIASED BIOLOGY 39
Biology Texts 39
Catastrophism 41
Vestigial Organs 42
Embryology 43
Biochemistry 44

4. THE BIBLE AND HISTORY 47
Historical References.. 47
The Discovery of Ebla 48
Eber 49
The Sons and Grandsons of Ebrium and Eber 49
What's in a Name? 50
Historical Sources 51
Elders in Ebla 53
The Sumerians... 55

5. IN THE BEGINNING 57
The First Period of Creation 57
The Second Period of Creation 60
The Miracle of Continents 62
Remarkable Accidents 63
Other Earths 65
Life on Other Earths.. 66
Spontaneous Life 67
Adam's Rib 68

6. INSTINCT 70
Genetically Controlled Behavior 71
Why Evolution.. 72
A Well Planned Operation 73
Mini-Creations.. 75
A Day of Rest? 76
Complex Behavior 77
Survival Skills 78
Human Instincts... 79
Human Sexuality 80
Homosexuality 81

7. ASSUMPTIONS AND CONCLUSIONS 84
New Concepts 84
Dark Age Reasoning 85
Assumptions that Simplify 85
Assumptions that Mystify 86

Testing Assumptions 87
False Assumptions 87
A Perplexing Problem 89
Reasoning of Prophets 91

8. FAITH AND KNOWLEDGE 93

Faith and Knowledge 93
The Testimony of Socrates 94
Research to Find God 96
The Depth of Hell 97

9. ETERNAL PROGRESSION 99

Spirit Matter 99
The Power of God 100
Creatures on Other Planets 102
Angelic Assignments 103
Priesthood in Heaven 104
Proof Without Certainty 105
Certainty Without Proof 106

10. RELATIVITY AND RESURRECTION 109

Governed by Light 109
Celestial Speed Limits 110
The Power of Resurrection 111
The Resurrection of Joseph Smith 112
Atoms of Resurrection 114
Adam and the Dust of the Earth 114
The Ultimate Set of Wheels 116

11. THE ATONEMENT 117

Mysteries 117
Receiving Revelation 118
Traditions 119
The Celestial Kingdom 121
Atonement Scriptures 122
A Righteous Judgement 123
Parallel Worlds 124
The Laws of Heaven 126

12. LIGHT AND GLORY 128
Forces 128
Spiritual Eyes and Ears 129
The Glory of God 130
Celestial Communication 131

13. IF YOU WERE GOD 134
The Joy of Discovery 134
The Language of Adam 134
Earliest Writing 135
The Confusion of Tongues 138
Neophyte Creators 141
Celestial Families 143

FOREWORD

This book offers a new perspective on man's involvment in the creation of the earth, the evolution of life, and Eternal progression. The nature of man's progression from man to God is explored from a Mormon point of view according to the author's understanding of the scriptures and available scientific evidence.

The controversy between evolution and special creation began with Darwin's book, *The Origin of Species,* written in 1859. National attention to this controversy was achieved in the Scopes trial in 1925 and the Seagraves vs. California trial in 1981. Several other state trials soon followed the California trial. In these, the creationists wanted teachers to give equal time to the biblical account of the creation. The courts generally decided that such a course was impractical as well as unconstitutional. For a time some states tried to force science teachers to teach the biblical account along with the standard evolutionary approach. For example, in 1974 Texas passed a law requiring that evolution be taught as "only one of several explanations." By April, 1984, Texas reinstated teaching evolution "as a theory" without need to mention creationists viewpoints. This was seen as a victory by the evolutionists.

The term "creationists," as used in this book, is defined as "one who believes that a Supreme Being created the world, as is understood by those who interpret the bible literally." The term "evolutionist" is defined as "one who believes that life began spontaneously in the oceans and evolved into all forms of earth life, past and present."

The first chapter contains a story of two doctors who give different diagnoses to a patient's ailment—they represent the viewpoints of the creationists and the evolutionists. The second chapter shows a great deal of harmony between special creation and evolution that proponents of the two theories seem to ignore. Chapter three presents examples of propaganda and cavalier atheistic statements currently found in some biology textbooks. Chapter four demonstrates that the Bible is an historical document. Chapter five shows that parallels exist between the account of the creation found in the Bible and the creation according to science. Chapter six examines complex behavior patterns which do not seem to be adequately explained by believers in evolutionary genetics. Chapter seven discusses both the benefits and the dangers which exist in making assumptions and in the use of logic. Chapter eight reminds us that faith is an integral part of all learning. Chapter nine discusses various elements of Eternal Progression.

Chapter ten investigates the possible effects of relativity on resurrected beings and discusses additional evidence of the existence of God. Chapter eleven explains how the atonement of Jesus Christ satisfies the demands of Justice and shows that Christ is the only redeemer. Chapter twelve discusses light, intelligence, and the glory of God, presenting evidence that God is aware of his creations throughout the universe. Chapter thirteen investigates the language of Adam and what happened at the Tower of Babel.

One reason this book was written was the tremendous sense loss I felt when an outstanding young man I knew lost his testimony while attending a university. We can be of little help to others if all we have to offer are platitudes when such a situation occurs. Do we ever ponder a principle long enough, or think it important enough to make a determined effort to explain it. We forget to notice the care with which ancient writers expressed themselves. Chiasmatic passages written by Lehi and others could not have been written without sober contemplations.

Disagreement concerning the time of creation and concerning the existence of pre-Adamic creatures has also occurred among some general authorities of the LDS Church. In 1930, Apostle Joseph Fielding Smith delivered a sermon titled *Faith Leads to a Fullness of Truth and Righteousness.* In this sermon he stated that geologists were misled by the evidence in the earth, that the earth was not as old as they claimed, that there was no life or death prior to Adam, and that pre-Adamic "men" did not exist.

B. H. Roberts took issue with those remarks, complaining that they had been published in a church magazine in a manner in which they would be perceived by readers as dogma from the church, rather than as an opinion expressed by an individual who was speaking officially for the Church. His concern was that the article was in error on many points which would adversely affect "the faith and status of a very large portion of the Priesthood and educated membership of the Church." (Letter to the Council of the Twelve dated April 5, 1930.) B. H. Roberts asked Joseph Fielding Smith for the source of his information. The answer was that he got it from the Bible.

After allowing both sides to present their cases to the Council of the Twelve, and finally to the First Presidency (Heber J. Grant was then president), the following was printed in the *Millennial Star* on February 19, 1931: "Leave Geology, Biology, Archaeology and Anthropology...to scientific research....We can see no advantage to be gained by a continuation of the discussion....Upon one thing we should all be able to agree, namely, 'Adam is the primal parent of our race.'"

B. H. Roberts died in 1933. *In Doctrines of Salvation,* Vol. I (1954) p. 80, Joseph Fielding Smith states: "We can hardly be justified in trying to harmonize the days of creation with extended periods of millions of years according to the reckoning of the so-called scientists." In his 1958 book *Answers to Gospel Questions*, Vol II, p. 191, he states, "It is doubtful that man will ever be permitted (by God) to make any instrument or ship to travel through space and visit the moon or any distant planet."

My fears are added to those of B. H. Roberts, that "The faith and status of a very large portion of the Priesthood and educated membership of the Church have been affected," because traditional views on the creation, held by a number of church members, have been taught in church settings. Viewpoints to the contrary have been viewed as somewhat apostate, not withstanding the publication of books such as *Science and Your Faith in God* (Bookcraft, 1928). The book is a selected compilation of writings by seven prominent LDS scientists. Frederick J. Pack, a geologist, discusses the creation time of the earth, and John A. Widtsoe acknowledges the existence of pre-Adamic beings and the geologic age of the earth. Perhaps the most outstanding book on this subject is *The Creation,* by Frank B. Salisbury (Deseret Book, 1976).

Biblical references in Genesis regarding Adam And Eve are known, in part, to be figurative. Christ taught in parables which have both superficial and profound meanings. If the profound meanings were sometimes misunderstood by the Apostles of his day (Mark 4:11), how much more careful must we be when using scriptures superficially in an effort to support our pre-conceived or traditional ideas.

FORWARD

A false theory can be countered only by concepts which are more consistent with available evidence. It is hoped that this book will cause some reflection on the inflexible positions which have been assumed by many evolutionists and creationists.

This book would have been a blessing to me during my high school and university years. The evidence for evolution seemed so overwhelming that there was little to be said except to live by faith. This bottom line of many LDS expositions on the subject does not, however, satisfy those who do not have a strong testimony or simply want to know more about the creation. Can scientific concepts help save a soul? They can if they build faith in God. Faith is the first step in any endeavor.

Chapter One
VIEWPOINTS

Two Points of View

A sixty-year-old doctor had a large, successful practice. Over ninety percent of his patients were impressed with his skill as a physician. As he was approaching retirement, he thought it would be wise to take in a partner. He therefore sought out a young doctor just beginning to practice medicine and soon found an applicant who met with his approval.

As he contemplated their partnership the older doctor thought, I have practiced medicine successfully for over thirty-five years and no doubt I shall be a valuable source of information to this new young doctor. I hope he will appreciate my experience. At the same time the younger doctor thought, I wonder if this old-timer knows the latest developments in medicine? I can be a real help to him on the newest diagnostic and surgical techniques.

A number of the older doctor's patients voluntarily transferred to the young doctor and the partnership got off to a good start. A short time later, a new patient arrived at the office. The nurse asked which doctor he wanted to see. He replied that he had a pain in his right side which really had him worried and would like to have the opinion of each doctor. The doctors in turn examined the patient. He had an elevated white blood cell count, pain and tenderness in his right side, a slightly elevated temperature, an occasional pain under his right scapula, nausea, and indigestion. After a preliminary examination, the two doctors announced their findings. The older doctor thought the patient might have appendicitis, but the young doctor suspected a bad gallbladder. Both agreed that further tests were necessary and that their patient should be hospitalized.

The following days were spent in the hospital with tests and x-rays. The doctors reviewed their findings each day but did not change their diagnoses. The antibiotics the patient was getting did not seem to stabilize his condition. Since the two doctors could not agree, they delayed operating one more day. The following day a laparotomy was performed. What they found was a double surprise: a ruptured appendix and a gangrenous gall-bladder. Due to the delay in operating, they nearly lost their patient.

In this parable, the two doctors represent people with preconceived notions who fail to appreciate another point of view. A common fault of many is that each sees his point of view as the only one possible. We often fail to realize that a point of view represents a vista from only one peak and others, standing on other peaks, can see things we are unable to see. Each point of view presents an incomplete picture.

Evolutionists

The parable refers to the concepts of evolutionists and creationists. Evolutionists are like the young doctor. They see chance evolution as the only possible explanation for the creation of life. They recognize that all the evidence is not in, but believe that they have enough to support their point of view unequivocally. They accept all evidence which supports their point of view and belittle the evidence which supports the existence of a supreme being. They are amazed by the order, majesty, and complexity of the universe and life on earth, but do not see a Master's touch, as did Einstein or Newton.

Some physicists suppose they will never discover a "first cause" in the creation of the universe, nevertheless they assume that it took place without need for an outside intelligence. Stephen Hawking, a leading Cambridge physicist, has proposed a *Principle of Ignorance* which says that an understanding of the first cause of the creation is ultimately unknowable.

Evolutionists treat the testimonies of the prophets in the Bible and *life after life* experiences of common people as fables and hallucination. They have no explanation for ethical man, or complex behavior in animals. (Some animal behavior is so predictable that you would think it was rehearsed before birth.)

Evolutionists use Einstein's theories and applaud his genius, but are embarrassed that his objection to Heisenberg's Uncertainty Principle was spiritual in nature. Einstein could not believe that God did not know the exact momentum and position of an atomic particle simultaneously. This is the basic postulate of the Uncertainty Principle. Einstein tried to find a flaw in the Uncertainty Principle, presenting several arguments against it to Niels Bohr. Each time, Bohr found a flaw in Einstein's argument. In his last attempt, Bohr was unable to find a flaw in Einstein's thought experiment until he made use of Einstein's own theory of relativity.

Einstein recognized that the Uncertainty Principle had a sound mathematical basis. Nevertheless, he stated his objection in these terms: "God does not play dice with the universe." The fact that Einstein did not succeed in finding a flaw in the Uncertainty Principle does not prove, or disprove the existence of God; it demonstrates Einstein's deep faith in a creator in face of apparent evidence to the contrary. It is interesting that some evolutionists infer that Einstein was an atheist because he did not go to church. Apparently it is important to them that this great scientific genius be on their side. This propaganda can be added to the list of biased or misleading statements made by evolutionists.

At this point, one may interject that it is not appropriate to chastise evolutionists for doing other than making objective scientific observations. If evolutionists did just that, this book may not have been written. Some examples of their non-objectivity will be seen in chapter three.

Many evolutionists seem to forget that scientific and historical concepts, well described by Hugh Nibley, "Have always been tentative, awaiting refinement from the latest body of evidence. Often the evidence comes as a surprise."[1] The corollary to this is that the mysteries of God are also revealed, on an individual basis, here a little and there a little and, as Joseph Smith found, sometimes as a surprise.[2]

---

[1] Hugh Nibley reveals a great deal about ancient concepts of the creation in books such as *The Timely and the Timeless*, Religious Studies Center, BYU., Ch. 2&3.

[2] Many were surprised when Joseph Smith revealed the 132nd section of the *Doctrine and Covenants* on plural marriage. An equal surprise was President Kimball's revelation on the priesthood being available to all worthy men. In each case, some church members were too steeped in tradition to accept new revelation. Tradition also prevented Joseph Smith from revealing other surprising principles. He said, "I have tried for a number of years to get the minds of the Saints prepared to receive the things of God," but "they will fly to pieces like glass as soon as anything comes that is contrary to their traditions: they cannot stand the fire at all." (TPJS, p. 331.) It is very possible that some of these revelations had to do with the creation.

Detractors do not understand this principle and suppose that no additions or clarifications could be made to the revelations published in the *Book of Commandments* which later became the *Doctrine and Covenants*.

Matter, Space and Time

In the parable the older doctor represents the creationists. They take the Bible to be literal (according to their interpretation). Some believe that the world and its family were created in six earth days. They use Genesis, Chapter One, as their proof, ignoring the statement in Chapter Two which states "These are the generations of the heavens and the earth in *the day* that the Lord created them." Others conclude that the word *day* must have a more general meaning, and allow a day to equal exactly one thousand years. Apparently *one thousand years* took up too much room on the written record and so *day* was used to save space. Others say that *day* must refer to an indefinite period of time, which is the view of many Bible readers today. If one wants Genesis, as well as the cosmic and geological record, to make sense, it appears that one must conclude that the word *day* does indeed have a more general meaning.

Many Latter-day Saints believe that we lived in heaven for an extremely long period of time before birth, long enough for 150 billion spirit brothers and sisters to be born. After spirit birth, we went through a long period of development and training.[3] Why would God want to create the earth quickly in 144 hours (six days), and deprive his children of participating in such an awesome and intricate process, when one purpose of this creation was so that his children could gain experience? Was Adam the only one who needed to learn about the process of creation?

It is true that the Lord explained that the day in which Adam would die was reckoned by the time of Kolob and was equal to one thousand years.[4] Does this mean that each time the Lord, or one of his Prophets, uses the word day, it can have only this meaning? Let us see how the Lord uses the word day in another scripture. In D & C 64:23 He said, "Behold, now it is called today until the coming of the Son of Man,

---

[3] Spencer W. Kimball, *Miracle of Forgiveness*, Bookcraft, pp. 4, 5.

[4] *Pearl of Great Price*, Abraham 3:4.

and verily it is a day of sacrifice, and a day for the tithing of my people." The word *day* in this passage does not mean one thousand years. It indicates a time for getting something done, rather than a period of specific duration. When God told Christ and Adam to create the world in stages, he did not tell them to work for one thousand years and then report on what had been completed. God told them what he wanted accomplished in each creative period and then to report back when that assignment was completed. That period of time was referred to as a day.

In some places, where the word *day* is expected to appear in the *Book of Abraham*, the word *time* appears instead. "And the Gods said among themselves, On the seventh time we will end our work, which we counseled."[5] "But of the tree of knowledge of good and evil, you shalt not eat; for in the time that thou eatest thereof, thou shalt surely die."[6]

One of Joseph Smith's associates, W. W. Phelps, published that the age of this system, according to Egyptian records, was 2.6 billion years old.[7] One possible significance of this number arises from the fact that Abraham explained principles of astronomy to the Egyptians.[8] This number is remarkable in that it is the first instance of a proposed age of the earth that is close to the present scientific estimate of 4.6 billion years old. I find no reference of church members at that time ridiculing the Egyptian statement as to the age of this system, although it is not clear what the Egyptians meant by *this system*.

These scriptures support the idea that the word *day*, as used in Genesis, is not always to be taken literally and that God, or a prophet, speaking in our idiom, may use a word in two places with two different meanings just as people today often do. Some continually insist that each statement God makes, through the language of his prophets, has the one literal meaning they envision, even after finding new meanings to seemingly literal terms such as *endless torment* and *eternal damnation*.[9] How the Lord taught in parables should be remembered.

---

[5] *Pearl of Great Price,* Abraham 5:2.

[6] *Pearl of Great Price, Abraham 5:13.*

[7] *Times and Seasons,* 5 Jan 1845.

[8] *Pearl of Great Price,* Facsimile #3.

One therefore should expect to find symbolism in other scriptures. The Lord used parables to decrease condemnation on those who did not understand and also to allow the joy of enlightenment to be received by those who pondered the deeper meanings.

Latter-day Saints believe in an omnipotent god who can travel rapidly through space. Therefore time must be different to Him according to relativity, and his own statement that "All is as one day with God and time only is measured unto men."[10] This statement is in agreement with physicists who state that matter, space and time had to be created together, and before that event took place, time did not exist. If the creation account in Genesis refers to the creation of the entire universe from a singularity in space (the big bang theory), it is no wonder that God simply said "In the beginning" he created the heavens and the earth.

The creation of diverse matter also automatically creates space and time. Space only exists between or around particles of matter. For instance, there is no space beyond the "edge" of the universe, if such a place exists. Can one contemplate heavens without celestial bodies, or earths without heavens? In D&C 88:37 we read; "And there are many kingdoms; for there is no space in the which there is no kingdom; and there is no kingdom in which there is no space, either a greater or lesser kingdom."

Time involves the position ordering of particles. The shortest duration of time depends on how quickly the most rapidly moving particles can change positions.[11] In special relativity, particles gain mass as they gain speed; consequently their ability to be accelerated and change positions decreases. This means that the time it takes for events to happen is increased, especially as their velocity approaches the speed of light. Physicists say that time is dilated, yet the time dilation is unnoticed by the rapidly moving creatures. Time is only noticed as being dilated by outside observers. Also, general relativity shows that time passes more slowly, near celestial bodies with great mass or when closer to a planet's surface. Quartz clocks tick slightly more slowly on earth than

---

[9] *D & C* Section 19.

[10] *Book of Mormon*, Alma 40:8.

[11] Notice how difficult it is to define time without using a time reference. In this case the word *quickly* was used to help with the definition.

when they are taken to the moon. If God uses a more slowly rotating, larger planet as a time reference, his time would be different not only because of the planet's rotation, but also because of its greater mass.

Thus matter, space and time are interrelated, and in fact cannot be separated. They exist together or not at all. Earth's time must, therefore, be different from God's time. Alma's statement (*Book of Mormon*, Alma 40:8), published in 1830—long before the advent of the concept of relativity in 1905—is in harmony with the idea that time may be different near a large celestial body such as Kolob or when God travels from one planet to another. Experiments have shown that Einstein's special and general relativities are accurate. His field equations are based on geometric surfaces and four dimensions (there may be more) but do not apply to all situations, such as in a black hole. Einstein states that "For large densities of field and matter, the field equations and even the field variables which enter into them will have no real significance."[12] Scientists do not presently use the term *theory of relativity*, they simply say relativity and treat it as an empirical fact.[13]

Creationists

Creationists skip lightly over such passages as: "Let the waters bring forth the creature that hath life, and the fowl that may fly..." Likewise, they hesitate to take the word *generations* too literally (...these are the generations of...); it sounds too much like evolution.

It appears odd that waters could bring forth fowl (which must be remarkable a statement to evolutionists, considering that it came from someone living in the bronze age: Moses), but this is exactly what scientists believe. Birds came from reptiles, which came from

---

[12] Albert Einstein, *The Meaning of Relativity, Fifth Edition.*, Princeton University Press, 1921, p. 129.

[13] Nothing in science is known to be absolutely correct. Relativistic calculations are the most accurate we can presently make in the practical world of space and time. Gravitational force is still a mystery. The other three forces, electromagnetic, and the strong and weak nuclear forces, are fairly well understood. The weak force disregards some laws followed by the strong and electromagnetic forces. It is predicted that the gravitational force may disregard even more laws than the weak force, and that when gravitational force predominates, such as in a blackhole, general relativity may no longer correctly describe relationships of space and time.

Nuclear forces were unknown in 1915, and Einstein did not include them in his explanation of general relativity. His field equations incorporate gravity and electromagnetic energy. Fortunately, nuclear forces are largely unimportant in calculations of space-time.

amphibians, which came from fish. Indeed, there is good agreement in the sequences of many of the events of the creation as seen by scientists and recorded in the Bible.

Taking a stand that the Bible is literally correct demonstrates, to some, allegiance to God. It seems such a simple thing to do. Just believe what the Bible says. This is what creationists say they are doing. Why, then, do they not agree on all points in the Bible, and also, why do they belong to hundreds of different Christian churches?

What do the creationists do with the scientific evidence that opposes their viewpoint? They use the evolutionists' solution. They ignore it. When confronted with the fossils found in the sediments, a typical creationist's response is, "The world is made from bits and pieces of other worlds which contained the fossils." Such remarks come from people who not only refuse to climb peaks to get a better look, but find security in the rut they are in. Yet these same "searchers for truth" believe that the glory of God is His intelligence. Their answer to the riddle of prehistoric man is simply that they were degenerate offspring of Adam. Radioactive dating and other evidences of fossil antiquity are brushed off as scientific hocus-pocus. Occasionally, when all else fails, opposing evidence is attributed to the work of Satan.

Can creationists know about things that have yet to be revealed to them in the manner prescribed by God? This prescription is the theme of *Science and Your Faith in God* which has been mentioned previously as well as D & C 88:79 and I Thess. 3:21.

Joseph Smith as a Scientist

Concepts that the earth was made from bits and pieces of other worlds may have come from a statement made by Joseph Smith that "The earth has been organized out of portions of other globes that have been disorganized."[14] Some imagine that the nonconformities and odd angles exhibited by the strata in the earth's crust are the result of piecing together the earth from other planets. But Joseph Smith went on to say that "God had materials to organize the world out of chaos—chaotic matter, which is element, and in the which dwells all the glory. Element had an existence from the time He had. The pure principles of element

---

[14] A. F. Ehat & L. W. Cook, *The Words of Joseph Smith,* Religious Studies Center, BYU, (1980), pp. 60, 61.

can never be destroyed: they may be organized and reorganized, but not destroyed."[15]

It is not clear from these references whether God is revealing information about the creation of the universe, our Milky Way galaxy, or the solar system—but it seems to point more to the creation of a galaxy or solar system. Galaxies are apparently not completely uniformly distributed throughout the universe, but may be found in clusters such as the thirty galaxies of our Local Group which are all small, except the Milky Way and our sister galaxy, Andromeda. In Abraham 3:3 we read; "These are the governing ones; and the name of the great one is Kolob, because it is near unto me, for I am the Lord thy God; and I have set this one to govern all those which belong to the same order as that upon which thou standest."

From this description, it seems likely that Kolob exists within the Milky Way Galaxy since it governs planets of the same order as the Earth. It is also possible that Kolob is in Andromeda which is larger than the Milky Way. Andromeda and the Milky Way govern the motions of all of the smaller galaxies in the Local Group. Page 111 discusses the possibility that Christ may have been involved in the creation of upwards of 200 million planet-earths within the Milky Way Galaxy. Notice that God does not live on Kolob, but near it. Kolob may be a gigantic blackhole and is refered to as a planet since it does not give off light but must have a great mass allowing it to control the motions of other planets and suns by its gravity.

Joseph Smith's statement does not say that God created the chaotic matter of which the world was made. This implies that God is a natural god rather than a supernatural god. Physicists cannot believe in a god who operates outside the laws of physics, but can accept a natural god who organizes existing materials.[16] This, however, begs the ultimate question: "Why does anything exist.?" (The only answer one can give to that question is, "Is it more likely that nothing should exist?")

Modern astronomers see stars eventually expanding to become red giants, then contracting to become white dwarfs or neutron stars. If

---

[15] Joseph Fielding Smith, *Teachings of the Prophet Joseph Smith*, Deseret Book, (1976), pp. 351, 352.

[16] Paul Davies, *God and the New Physics*, Simon & Schuster, 1983, p. 209.

the stars are large enough, they contract further and then explode as a supernova.[17] The scattered elements from the exploding supernova are gathered again by gravity, along with space dust and gas to form another solar system. Our solar system matter, according to this type of evidence, has already been recycled.

Our solar system was organized about five billion years ago in the Milky Way galaxy, which is estimated to be about fifteen billion years old. It has orbited the center of our galaxy about twenty times since its creation, but it may have been in a somewhat different position than it is now. There are some places, such as globular clusters, or near the center of the galaxy, where planetary life could not exist because of the intense radiation. The oldest stars in our galaxy are over ten billion years old, but many are younger, and all of the massive stars that existed in the beginning have long since exploded.

Massive stars quickly burn out and explode as a supernova to supply neighboring space with the materials needed to form a living solar system. (And as one earth shall pass away, and the heavens thereof, even so shall another come.[18]) Life as we know it could not exist during the first billion years of the life of a galaxy since few heavy elements existed, and nearly everything was made of hydrogen and helium. The fact that the earth contains heavy atoms like uranium and lead is strong evidence that the earth's elements were created during the last stages of previously existing stars.

Thus we see that Joseph Smith's statement that the pure principles of element are eternal, and that the earth has been organized out of portions of other disorganized globes, is in good company with present scientific evidence, though it was without precedent in 1830.

In 1803 John Dalton proposed a theory that atoms were the basis of matter and could not be broken down. The ministers of that era declared that God created the world out of nothing (ex nihilo).[19]

---

[17] There is a stage of expansion and contraction in the life of large stars each time the major source of energy shifts to a heavier element, such as from hydrogen to helium or from helium to carbon.

[18] Moses 1:38.

[19] Question: What signifies the words creation of heaven and earth?
Answer: They signify that God made heaven and earth and all creatures in them of nothing, by his word only. (Douay Roman Catholic Catechism)

Joseph Smith's statements in 1830 and 1841 about the eternal nature of the pure principles of the elements was in the forefront of scientific thought of his day. When Joseph Smith was born, conservation of mass was just beginning to be understood.

Chemists such as Antoine Lavoisier, in a 1789 text, provided evidence that mass is conserved in chemical reactions. Now (after Einstein), scientists say that mass-energy is conserved, since mass can be converted into energy and vise-versa. Notice that Joseph Smith's statement allows for that. Instead of saying that elements were eternal, as the scientists were beginning to say, he said that the pure principles of element are eternal. To illustrate how little was known about atoms in 1841, one must remember that the electron was not discovered until 1897. It was not until the 20th century that astronomers began theorizing about the creation and death of solar systems.

Our Educational Limits

When I was in high school, our English teacher assigned the class to read Wordsworth's *Intimations of Immortality*. We were to be prepared to discuss the poem the next day in class. I was a little dismayed when I saw the length of the poem, but I proceeded to read it that evening. As I read the first stanza, the words *celestial light* caught my attention and I began to read it with more interest. When I read the fifth stanza I was so impressed that I reread it several times

> Our birth is but a sleep and a forgetting
> The soul that rises with us, our life's star,
> Hath had elsewhere its setting
> And cometh from afar:

> Not in entire forgetfulness,
> And not in utter nakedness,
> But trailing clouds of glory do we come
> From God, who is our home.

The verse was so profound and beautiful I thought it would be well to memorize it. I started to do so when another thought ran through my mind: this is not part of your assignment; you don't need to memorize this stanza; you had better spend your time reading the rest of the poem. I struggled for a moment with that decision when another thought struck me: do I only learn what I am told to learn? Have I been limiting my education to what others think I ought to know? When am I going to take the responsibility for my own development? This feeling was reinforced when I read from the seventh stanza:

> As if his whole vocation
> Were endless imitation.

I had been doing the same thing in church, and learning very little. I began to realize how little I really knew when I was assigned as a junior home teaching companion to Robert J. Matthews, presently dean of Religious Education at Brigham Young University. But what really brought the message home was two years later when I was in the U. S. Navy stationed at Long Beach California. One Sunday I looked up the address of the nearest LDS ward, took a bus, walked a few blocks, and arrived at what looked like an LDS church building. I quickly went inside and found the members already in Sunday School classes. I found a class of adults and sat near the back of the room. I was glad to be there and anticipated enjoying the discussion that was going on. That anticipation quickly turned to bewilderment. The things they were discussing were going right over my head. They were discussing things completely foreign to me, and everyone else seemed to understand what was going on.

I began to wonder if I had wandered into the wrong church. After a few more minutes of the same, I quietly walked out to look more carefully at the name of the church over the front door. I was stunned when I read, "The Church of Jesus Christ of Latter-day Saints." A very subdued church member walked quietly back to class pondering his ignorance. I began to study the scriptures in earnest and made up my mind to read the standard works before my enlistment was over. I tell this story as a reminder that the road to learning is an uphill climb, not a leisurely stroll. Up to that time, my faith in the church was based primarily upon the faith of my parents. It was during my three year enlistment that I studied the Book of Mormon and found out that it was true.

The conflict between the concepts of evolution and special creation is experienced by nearly everyone attending a university. When I was in that setting a few years later, I thought that I ought to take a class in anthropology to see if there was much substance to the arguments of the evolutionists. I found that the class barely scratched the surface.

Looking for a peak to climb to get a better view, I was left on a foothill. Later I studied the development of the earth in seven geology classes. This gave me the opportunity to examine strata and collect fossils from many formations in Utah. These studies, combined with others such as anatomy, biochemistry, biophysics, chemistry, embryology, genetics, microbiology, physics, physiology, radiobiology and zoology, finally allowed me to climb the paleontological mountain high enough to get a more complete picture of evolution. Evolution did, and does take place.

Speciation, One Form of Evolution

One form of evolution, called speciation, has always existed and continues to operate in all living organisms. It helps offspring adapt to new conditions and is an operation inherent in genes. That is, genetic material is organized so that speciation takes place randomly without further direction. But, in my opinion, speciation alone was not responsible for past phylogenetic evolution.

Speciation is a permanent anatomical or physiological change brought about by a genetic mutation which still allows interbreeding with related species containing the same compliment of genes. If species are separated, speciation may continue until interbreeding no longer takes place due to altered mating displays or genetic incompatibility. The jury is still out on the cause of the appearance of different classes and families of living things with attendant major chromosomal changes. Evolutionists see this phylogenetic evolution as an extrapolation of speciation. Extrapolation is risky business. It is a theory which has never been demonstrated. No one has observed an additional new gene added to a chromosome in a naturally occurring macroscopic organism. A gene transplanted from another organism is not considered here to be a new gene. This difficult observation may require the chromosomes in the organism to be completely mapped.

This is not to say that some naturally occurring phylogenetic evolution did not take place. Some LDS scientists believe that all plants and animals developed spontaneously from a single living cell.[20] But, one

---

[20] We read of the ancient belief that Atlas held up the world, standing on a turtle, which was swimming in a sea. Then we smile and ask, "What is holding up the sea?" We teach that living organisms are made of organs, which are made of tissues, which are made of cells. The ancients could well smile and ask for the origin of the cells.

should be aware of what is theory and what is fact. Those who believe that phylogenetic evolution and speciation are the same thing illustrate evolution by the development of a new species. The author believes that genetic mutation was extremely useful in the evolution of living things, but it was only one of the methods used by God. The most common solution to the problem is that God created living things by evolution. If this solution includes the random-chance concept held by evolutionists, it is incorrect.

Speciation involves the mutation of single genes. Evolution, on the other hand, requires additional new genes, not just alteration of existing genes, just as it requires more to build a new addition on a house than to change wallpaper and rearrange furniture in one of your rooms. Speciation is rearranging furniture, evolution involves adding a new wing. The begged question is, how are new, additional, genes produced? To make it worse, they must be produced in batches. For example, genetic research has uncovered some of the secrets of the genes that make insulin. Scientists can see when it first appeared in living things, but do not as yet understand how it was first created along with the other genes necessary to control the storage of sugar and regulate its level in the blood.[21] This is a little like contemplating the invention of the bow and arrow. One man fashions a bow for no apparent reason, then sets it in the corner since it is of no use to him. Meanwhile another man constructs an arrow, while another makes a bowstring, and yet another fashions feathers and sets them aside since they also are of no use. Then one day . . . .

The other side of the issue requires spiritual research. The scriptures are the best place to start. From the scriptures one learns that the inspiration of the Holy Ghost is promised to those who seek the truth. The temple is also a place where one gets his bearings on creation

---

[21] Insulin is produced by the islets of Langerhans, in the pancreas, when the blood sugar level gets too high. This is done by a complex sequence of steps beginning with a gene that makes preproinsulin. Parts of the preproinsulin chain are discarded while other parts are recombined, by other genetically produced cleaving enzymes and receptors, producing proinsulin and eventually insulin. Glucagon is also genetically engineered to counteract insulin and raise the level of blood sugar if it gets too low. Finally, somato statin is produced to shut down the entire operation of the islet cells if needed.

See Scientific American, Sept. 1988, page 89, for a diagram of this complex operation, and ask yourself if you think this was a genetically engineered creation by an intelligent being or a chance event.

and evolution, but one must go there to understand what is meant by this statement.

It may well be that the creationists have read into the scriptures things that are not there, and the evolutionists have read into the geological record things that are not there. Each have a shaky footing in only allowing one viewpoint. If we go back to the example of the two doctors, we find that each was partially correct in his diagnosis and partially incorrect. The patient, seeking the truth, turns to each, is confused by their lack of agreement, and because of each intractable opinion, the patient is nearly lost. Is it possible that the same thing could be true of the evolutionists and creationists? Is it also possible to take evidence from each and develop an explanation that might lie closer to the truth?

Chapter Two
THE CREATION OF LIFE

The Origin of Species

On a journey around the world, Darwin studied animals and plants in many places. On the Gallapagos Islands, he observed a variety of finches of different sizes, shapes of beaks and habitats. He concluded that they all evolved from a single species of finches that arrived shortly after the volcanic islands were formed. Such observations were the basis for his book on evolution, *The Origin of Species by Means of Natural Selection.*

The development of these varieties of finches demonstrates one form of evolution. Each of the 13 species of finches found on the islands is adapted to a particular niche, has different physical characteristics, and interbreeding may no longer be possible among all species. Due to the recent formation and isolated position of the Gallapagos Islands, Darwin's conclusion that the finches descended from a single species is nearly inescapable. There is no question that genetic changes have taken place. But an equally important question is, "What was the nature of those genetic changes?" Were additional genes produced or were existing genes simply altered? One may ask, "What difference does it make as long as a change was produced?"

It is a natural, but speculative, conclusion that because a small change can occur to create a new species, the changes continue spontaneously until a new genus is developed. Although this may be a correct assumption, it has not yet been demonstrated. In a similar manner, the resistance of bacteria to antibiotics and the mutations of the fruit fly have been presented as evidence of evolution. But genetic evolution must eventually produce a chromosomal change that not only prevents

THE CREATION OF LIFE

interbreeding with the old species, but also demonstrates the addition of genes.

The genetic code uses a triad of nucleotide bases, called a codon, which are able to assemble specific amino acids. Three special bases are used out of a selection menu of four.[1] Computers often use an octet of binary digits for code. Genes are like a page or subroutine of a computer program, or like a macro in a word processor. Suppose you made a robot with arms and legs with a video camera for an eye. You ask two programmers to write a program for each function, such as walking or picking up an object. The programs for these functions would require many subroutines and the total program might be quite lengthy. The program each programmer writes is analogous to a chromosome, while each page or subroutine is analogous to a gene. You then program the computer to select the walking, detecting, or hand movement program that is easiest to run, the dominant program.

The program may be so long that it must be stored on a magnetic disc. The robot calls forth each program as it needs it, although it may have enough memory to keep two programs active at the same time. During the storage and retrieval of a program, the computer may develop an error due to mechanical or electrical problems. When the program with the error is run, say for picking up an object, the robot will fail to accomplish that task. A parity check could detect the error, cause the computer to reject the dominant program, call forth the other program, the recessive one, and try again.

Gene duplication in sex cells may also develop mechanical or electrical problems and cause a mutation. A mutation is an error in the exact duplication of a gene in a reproductive cell, producing a gamete or offspring. Both radiation and heat can cause errors in computer memory chips as well as genes. But errors can sometimes be corrected. Memory chips now compensate for defective areas by using spare locations. There is evidence that the nervous system also has spare neurons. A base pair check occurs in the sex cells when sperm and

---

[1] In RNA, the number of combinations of three bases out of a selection menu of four (A,U,C,G) is 64, since the bases may be used more than once. However, only 20 amino acids are actually produced. For instance (GUA) produces the amino acid valine. Our body is able to manufacture 10 amino acids and must depend on plants or animals for the other ten. Of the 64 codons, one (AUG) tells the cell where to begin protein synthesis and three others (UAA, UAG, or UGA) tell it where to stop.

egg unite to ensure that proper fertilization is taking place. A base pair check on an incorrectly copied gene in a DNA chain also takes place and can lead to a genetic error correction even after the DNA chains recombine.[2]

Mutations

Some chemicals, like colchicine, have the ability to cause a double set of chromosomes to be produced. This is called polyploidy and is a mutation which is sometimes beneficial in plants. It has improved such crops as blueberries, wheat, and McIntosh apples. In most creatures, extra genes are generally harmful, such as in Down's syndrome. The harm is usually due to the overproduction or repression of essential organic molecules.

None of the mutations mentioned has yet been shown to produce a new genus, which generally requires additional new genes, not duplication, transfer, or mutation of old genes. A retrovirus may transfer an existing gene from one organism to another causing such things as AIDS. What mutations are not certain to do is increase the gene pool necessary to create a new genus.

If you wanted to add an additional capability to the robot, such as the ability to accept word commands, you would have to write an additional program and add additional parts. How likely is it that you could accidently come up with such a program made from bits and pieces of a previous program, or from a previous program that developed errors in just the right places? This is what evolutionists believe happened to genes as life progressed from the first miraculous living cell to man.

---

[2] A parity check in a computer is a count to see if a given number of elements is odd or even. In cells, replicating RNA is subjected to three different quality control mechanisms. The enzymes that perform these checks can even tell which half of a replicated DNA strand is the original by examining each strand for methyl groups. Although we can easily see that a parity check in a computer could only be accomplished by intelligent programming, evolutionists see nothing wrong with the incredibly precise nature of the rejection of wrong bases happening by accident in nature which flies in the face of reason when one looks at the complex series of actions shown in the diagrams. This is detailed in *Scientific American*, August 1988, p. 40 which states, "As is seen in so many other biological systems, the balance between flexibility and precision in DNA replication is a delicate, complex and subtle product of billions of years of evolution." Although there is not one shred of evidence that this mechanism was the product of spontaneous evolution, evolution, as always, gets the credit—showing how ingrained it is in the thought processes of scientists.

Mutations have produced many new species during recorded history. As a matter of fact, all bears have been traced to a common ancestor in Asia. But, like the finches on the Galapagos, such species mutations have never as yet led to the formation of a new genus. The usual explanation for this is that we have not been around long enough to observe it—it can clearly be seen in the fossil record. But what evidence exists that the fossil record is a product of speciation? Until recently, one might have argued that there is no other way to cause evolution. But now we have genetic engineering.

There are an estimated 100,000 genes in a mammalian cell but only about 2,000 in a bacterium. If we allow 600,000,000 years for the development of man, beginning with the Cambrian period, we discover that a new gene must be added to the mammalian line about every 6,000 years. If we consider 1,000 mammals, from aardvarks to zebras, probability requires that an additional new gene be developed in one of these animals about every six years. This does not seem to be happening. Also, the same sets of genes that have been added to animals in the geologic past have also been added to different classes of animals in what is termed parallel evolution. This seems unexplained by random mutations that should have produced many more kinds of physiological systems and organs than presently observed.

It is hard to say how many genes must be added before a new phenotype is observed. (This is a species with a significant change in anatomy.) A gene may relate to the metabolism within a cell rather than a skeletal change that can be seen. Genetic mutations in humans, such as the trait for sickle cell anemia, are changes in only one nucleotide of a DNA chain. Dozens of nucleotides are usually needed to make a gene.

The following statement was made by Donald Johnson, curator of anthropology and director of scientific research at the Cleveland Museum of Natural History:

> Homo erectus existed essentially unchanged for 1.5 million years and then suddenly Homo sapiens emerged, but we don't know why. (1980 Cottam Natural History Lecture, University of Utah.)

Evolutionary Jumps

"Evolutionists agree that species tend to last for long periods of geological time and that when a new species is created, it is by a sudden jump. The mechanism for these evolutionary changes is not completely understood and is presently being debated by evolutionists." (*Science,* August 28, 1981)

In an article titled *Enigmas of Evolution,*[3] which featured paleontologist Stephen Jay Gould, we read:

> Darwin, and those who followed him, believed that the work of evolution was slow, gradual and continuous and that a complete lineage of ancestors, shading imperceptibly one into the next, could in theory be reconstructed for all living animals. In practice, Darwin conceded, the fossil record was much too spotty to demonstrate those gradual changes, though he was confident that they would eventually turn up.
>
> But a century of digging since then has only made their absence more glaring. Paleontologists have devoted whole careers to looking for examples of gradual transitions over time, and with a few exceptions they have failed....
>
> In 1972, Gould and colleague Niles Eldrege proposed to call off the official search and accept the evidence of the fossil record on its own terms. Rather than transform gradually, most of the species in the world appear to have evolved relatively quickly and to have persisted, virtually unchanged, for millions of years.
>
> By mechanisms not yet understood, new species appear to split off at random from existing ones. If they have some advantage, they may in time supplant their ancestors, although it is also possible that both species will coexist for a long time—until, as usually happens, a major change in the environment wipes out one or both of them.
>
> The rule applies to Homo sapiens as it does to other species. Stephen M. Stanley, a Johns Hopkins paleontologist, presents in a recent book (*The New Evolutionary Timetable,* Basic Books) the idea that human beings did not evolve by the gradual growth

---

[3] *Newsweek,* March 29, 1982

of the brain from one generation to the next but, discontinuously....Moreover, we can no longer view ourselves as the perfect result of testing and refinement going back 3 million years to 'Australopithecus.'

For all the excitement it has generated, punctuated equilibrium (as the theory is called) still smacks of heresy to many scientists. It does not explain what many regard as the crucial point: how and why a new species springs up.

It is an interesting exercise to estimate the number of evolutionary steps required to produce the total number of genera alive and extinct. Perhaps 10 billion is reasonable. The number of species steps is, of course, many times greater. Presently there are about thirty million known living species on earth. A rough calculation of the number of steps (n) is to let $2^n = 10^{10}$. In this estimate, n would be about 26. If each evolutionary step began with a new gene and if each old gene added a gene at the same rate, you would end with some 26 genes chains of various length. The longer the gene chain, the more primitive its origin. The gene chains are chromosomes.

Although genes can occasionally change locations on a chromosome, it would be interesting to see if the sequence of genes in a chromosome would help trace the phylogenetic development of a species. Evolutionists talk of evolution as being a series of progressive steps, the only guiding power being the genes' desire to survive. The reason we see forms of life of increasing complexity during the history of the earth, according to evolutionists, is to help insure the survivability of the genes. It would be true that competition would continually require more advanced bodies, just as in war the best equipped armies win the battle.

There are some who contend that spontaneous evolution disobeys the Second Law of Thermodynamics, but we continually receive energy from the sun making spontaneous evolution remotely possible. Besides, the whole universe disobeys this law. No one can explain how the universe got wound up. It seems to be like a clock that was wound up and has been running for 16 billion years with a definite end in sight—which is called the heat death of the universe. If one wishes a moment of silence to occur, one has only to ask a scientist who wound up the universe. At the present time the universe is less than half-way wound down for living organisms.

If our robot lost the program to interpret word commands, we would be left with a robot that only walked and picked up objects. Perhaps devolving animals would simply not survive but neither should evolving animals. When outside genes are added to a cell by a retrovirus, bad things usually happen. Speciation allows development of different subspecies to fill different niches in the environment, but they are apparently due to alterations in existing genes.

Advanced forms of life are not necessarily better prepared to survive. Sharks are primitive, but survive very well without need for improvement because they have few enemies with better equipment. But if one group of ancient hominids were masters of all others, why did their genes feel that improvement was still needed for their security?

Longevity of Man

As one examines the genetic mutations of man and the increase in birth defects, one gets the impression that their genes are less perfect than those of their parents, who had genes less perfect than their parents.[4] This would continue back to Adam. The longevity of the human body is certainly related to its physiology, which is under the control of the genes in each cell. What other explanation can you give for the fact that Adam and his generation lived for nearly 1,000 years? After the Biblical flood, the longevity of man decreased to 400 years and finally to less than 100 years.

Thus, one gets the impression that Adam and Eve started out with perfect genes. The seed of death that they passed on to their offspring may have been a gene mutation they received when they partook of the forbidden fruit. There is no mention of the reluctance to marry a near relative until after the Biblical flood. By that time the human race had developed enough mutations to make such marriages risky for child bearing. If one were able to create a genetically perfect individual, it is possible that such a person would not age, and live indefinitely. A genetic engineer who could do this might then have discovered the secrets of the *Tree of Life*.[5] Would God want to prevent such a discovery?

---

[4] One may well argue that we are only more aware of different birth defects today because of our ability to help such babies survive.

[5] "And now, lest he put forth his hand and partake also of the tree of life, and eat and live forever. Therefore I, the Lord God, placed...cherubim and a flaming sword, which turned every way to keep (guard) the way of the tree of life." (*Pearl of Great Price,* Moses 4:28-31)

Here indeed is a paradox to evolutionists. As time goes on, the human species seems to acquire a greater variety of detrimental mutations. Realizing that 4,000 B.C. is only 1/100,000 of the way back to the Cambrian era, our progenitors in 4000 B.C. should have had about the same number of genetic defects that we have now—the difference would only be 0.001%. But their recorded longevity is evidence that this is not the case, and that their origin was not through evolution but required a special creation. The evolutionists response is that they really did not live that long. Perhaps the writers of the Bible anticipated the importance of the longevity of the antedeluvians in supporting the creationists viewpoint and expanded their ages accordingly.

We have evidence of evolution and special creation. The rules seem to be that you can choose only one. They must be mutually exclusive. Doctors also like their patients to have one affliction at a time. Can one accept the idea that evolution and special creation may coexist or that the evolutionary record is a record containing both spontaneous and genetically engineered creations?

Adam as a Creator

According to LDS doctrine, God instructed Christ and Adam to cause plants and animals to develop on the earth beginning with the simplest types.[6] Evolutionary tendencies were apparently built into the genetic material which allowed slow evolutionary changes to take place and new species to form to cope with different environments. (This corresponds to Darwin's survival of the fittest concept.) This is now more correctly described as the survival of the fitter, since living things flourish only if they fit into the environment. If these evolutionary tendencies could add genes and develop chromosomes, why would not God just sit back and let this spontaneous evolution create all the plants and animals of the earth, including man?

The benefit of longevity in the beginning was a definite help as the human race was getting started and learning how to do things. Evolution does not seem to provide for this. Another answer to the question in

---

[6] The Priesthood was first given to Adam....He obtained it in the Creation, before the world was formed. (TPJS, p. 157.) Adam's priesthood was then functioning prior to and during the creation. Bruce R. McConkie states that "Under Christ (Adam) participated in the creative enterprise." (*Mormon Doctrine,* p.16.) This is implied in Abraham 3:22-26.

the above paragraph will be given later, but for now ask yourself, "Why does a teacher have lesson plans?" Why not just follow the path where the discussions lead?

God has a specific scope and sequence ordered in the creation. This requires that the evolutionary tendencies built into living things did not get out of hand. From time to time, more advanced forms were added by Adam, who was assisted, in an apprentice capacity, by God's other children. This was done, not because it was impossible to have created them by spontaneous evolution, but to keep pace with the spiritual creation and give God's children experience in the creation of living things.

At the end of each creative period, God tells us that he "Saw that all things were good."[7] This is in harmony with the idea that God was observing the creative efforts of others, that some variation was possible, and that it was controlled to meet his specifications. It is possible that some genera and families were created by spontaneous evolution. That would make it unnecessary to genetically engineer or transplant every variety of plant and animal. In either case, it would leave a fossil record that still required faith to believe in God.

Would evolution and creation on other living planets create an identical set of plants and animals? Not as long as artists like to create new and different pictures. Creators like to create, not copy. The primary creation was, however, spiritual. If all things were first created spiritually, how could the physical creation correspond to it if plants and animals were randomly created by chance? What would spirit bears do if evolution on the physical earth did not produce bears? The physical creation had to be controlled to correspond to the preceding spiritual creation.

Many believe that man (Adam) was on earth before the animals and therefore no evolution was possible. In the *Pearl of Great Price,* we read that man became "the first flesh upon the earth."[8] If Christ and Adam created the earth under God's direction, Adam had to be

---

[7] Genesis 1:21.

[8] *Pearl of Great Price,* Moses 3:7. God refers to Adam as the first man on earth. Therefore, Adam was not born while his parents were on the earth. Otherwise, his parents would have been first. How, then, was Adam made from the dust of the earth? See the chapter on relativity and resurrection for a possible solution to this paradox.

the first flesh on the earth. Christ at this point existed as a spirit, but Adam had to have a physical body in order to later become the father of the human race. When certain plants and animals were needed on the earth, it was likely Adam who was given that assignment. Some suppose that he would have obtained them from the planet on which he previously lived and all planets would have the same animals—in contradiction to footnote #8 on page 102. This is not the most productive method. The most productive method is to create them by genetic engineering, allowing each of us creative experiences.

A major genetic change in a plant or animal would leave a gap in the fossil record. Such gaps may indicate that the creators did not feel it necessary to minimize each evolutionary step, but too many major genetic changes would be counterproductive to giving God's children opportunities to create new or advanced life forms and to living by faith. Most gaps in the fossil record may be the natural consequence of the limited numbers of fossils preserved and collected, but some real gaps apparently exist, as noted on page 30.

Suppose we were to discover a new kind of ape that looked more like man and could even talk on a two-year-old level. Would that make us feel uncomfortable? "These two facts exist, that there are two spirits, one being more intelligent than the other; there shall be another more intelligent than they; I am the Lord thy God, and am more intelligent than they all." (Abr. 3:19.)

Pre-Historic Man

Degrees of intelligence exist on a continuum from God on one end to the amoeba on the other. Would it be unreasonable to find fossils of man-like creatures that appeared to be less intelligent than man, but more intelligent than apes? During the sixth creative period, if prehistoric man-like creatures were living, how would Adam respond if he were asked if man had yet evolved? His answer would be no![9] The only proper way for God's children to be born on the earth is as offspring of God's children.

---

[9] Pre-Adamic hominids were not considered "men" by God, but this does not denigrate their existence. Our relationship to them and the animals is still somewhat of a mystery. The intelligence of spirits determines what kind of a body they will posses. We are told that celestial bodies will also differ from terrestrial and telestial bodies. (D & C 76:70.)

What does the future hold for these pre-Adamic "men" and "women" of lower intelligence who have filled the measure of their creation and obeyed the laws of the kingdom to which they belonged?[10] No matter what kingdom one belongs to, there need to be those standing on higher ground who are willing to impart of their wisdom and provide growth opportunities for those seeking their fellowship and help. There also needs to be opportunities to be a blessing and give direction to those with less understanding.[11] Who will care for the animals?

What should one do with intelligences that were less than human but greater than apes—or would it be better to forbid such intelligences to exist? One may imagine that those animals we loved and cared for on the earth will want to be with us again in a kingdom of glory, but who will have time to care for the millions of unknown animals who will live in the forests of those kingdoms? One possible answer is the Cro-Magnon, Neanderthal and other hominids.

Not having the intelligence to make celestial covenants and creations, they will find joy and growth in caring for animals under the direction of God's children. In the economy of operation in God's kingdom, hominids were a necessary creation! We should not regard them with anything but benevolence. They are our friends. In their pre-existence, they undoubtedly helped the higher animals learn survival skills. (See the chapter on instinct.) It was necessary that they precede Adam's posterity so that they would not be abused and also to provide "missing links" so that man's relation to God would be based on faith.

For some reason, many imagine that the creation of worlds, plants, and animals is God's primary vocation. Then after gaining satisfaction from these endeavors, he created man and allowed him to live on one of his created worlds. But this idea is in conflict with God's statement that his children are his work and his glory.[12] God's primary vocation is making it possible for his children to find joy in doing the things he has done, including the creation of worlds and living things.

---

[10] "And unto every kingdom is given a law; and unto every law there are certain bounds also and conditions. All beings who abide not in those conditions are not justified." (*D & C* 88:38-39.)

[11] Celestial beings minister to terrestrial beings and they in turn minister to telestial beings. To whom do telestial beings minister? For a surprising answer see the last page of chapter eight.

[12] *Pearl of Great Price*, Moses 1:39.

In order for a spirit child of God to function in the flesh, the spirit must be placed in a body with a brain that corresponds to its own intelligence. This is why the spirit children of God would never be placed in the bodies of a sub-human species. Pre-historic hominids who lived before the Garden of Eden were not intelligent enough to be the chosen vessels for God's spirit children. When we compare the cranial capacity of Homo sapiens (1300 cc) to those of Homo erectus (900 cc) and Homo hablis (650 cc) we can see why this was the case. Even Neanderthals and Cro-Magnon were inappropriate vessels.

> Eric Trinkaus of the University of New Mexico has shown that the Neanderthals (and probably their contemporaries in other parts of the Old World) were probably as unlike us behaviorally as they were physically. . . . Important behavioral changes are evident in the archaeological record....All of this points to the emergence of a species possessing modern behavioral capabilities (and potential) from an ancestral species lacking, at least by modern standards, in some significantly human characteristics. (Scientific American, March 1984, p. 96.)

The Final Quarter of the Senior Year

In this chapter we see that it is possible that all evolutionary steps were not the result of random gene mutation, such as appears to take place in speciation. Speciation may, or may not, be random. Some speciation may be the result of intelligent genetic engineering. Evolutionary gaps, or jumps, really seem to exist.

The evolutionary jumps, and the longevity of Adam, indicates that special creations have occurred. It is hard to picture God being involved in billions of minuscule special creations every time a new genus of plant of animal appeared on earth. But how elevating it is to imagine that God's 150 billion spirit children were doing exactly that—as they learned to create, one step at a time.

The idea that God created all plants and animals through the evolutionists scenario of random gene mutations, after placing the first living cell in an ocean, is in conflict with Genesis which states that God labored for six days to create the earth and its living things. The evolutionists scenario would require God to do nothing after creating the first cell. This would be a tragedy of the greatest magnitude since it would deprive God's children of an avenue of progression and the exciting opportunity of creating plants and animals found no where else in the universe.

Some examples of how we may have been involved in the creation will be given in chapter six. One must keep in mind that if we failed to get involved in the creation of the earth and its living creatures, we would have wasted a golden opportunity for progression. There is no reason to suppose that such a stage in our development is to take place in the future—on the contrary, our present earthly experience seems to be the final quarter of the Senior Year.

Chapter Three
BIASED BIOLOGY

Biology Texts

Astute students are likely to be offended by the presentations on evolution in many biology texts. The authors should present evidences of evolution without making unscientific judgments about the folly of special creation. Some writers seem to be guided by the following illogic.

> Premise: Either God or evolution created life.
> Observation: Evolution exists.
> Conclusion: Evolution created life and God does not exist.

The premise, implied in many biology texts, is faulty. There is no reason to suppose that God and evolution are mutually exclusive. Some writers give you the impression that, as detectives, they would have to catch a thief in the act before they would make an arrest. Yet nearly all scientific conclusions are based on probability and inductive evidence. There is a great deal of inductive evidence that God exists. Is it proper to accept one source of inductive evidence and reject another? Do evolutionists have to set up straw men to win their arguments?

The reader must realize that the author's complaints are directed to the authors of certain biology texts. Some specific examples will now be given. Below, and on the next four pages, the reader will find statements made in biology texts from a Utah high school. The first book is *The Study of Biology* (Addison-Wesley).

> There are three general kinds of explanations for the wide diversity of form in the living world. The first is the idea of 'special

creation,' which holds that species arose in the past as the result of a supernatural act. At the time of creation, these species possessed exactly the same characteristics as they do today.

The author of the biology text has taken a great deal of liberty in writing the last sentence above. It seems to have been written so the student would logically reject special creation. It is an outlandish, strawman amendment to the idea that God was the creator.

There may be some creationists without scientific training who believe that after the creation, no further species changes took place. But for some biology text authors to make it look as if this is the official position of creationists, is nothing short of propaganda. Few science students with creationist leanings would be in this extremist position.

In their book, the authors constantly remind the student not to make unwarranted statements that assign an anthropomorphic purpose to an action. Now consider one of their own statements.

> Given the alternative theory of special creation, it would be necessary to suppose that the Creator whimsically allowed some species to perpetuate themselves while causing others to die off. The fact that there are many more extinct species than presently alive on earth would indicate that the Creator's whims must have been rather frequent.

The authors' statement above is about as anthropomorphic as you can get, describing God's methods and character in terms of human frailties. They also state:

> The mixing of science and religion is always unfortunate, for it makes objective weighing of the evidence pro and con virtually impossible; the emotional attachments are simply too strong.

One must wonder about the objectivity of the authors of such statements. What is the source of their emotional attachments to prove that God does not exist? Are they too proud to accept the idea that someone more intelligent may exist? They label the reasoning of the science student who believes in God as 'always unfortunate', and try to show that the student who has persisted in believing in God believes in a whimsical God. One might expect such texts in Russia but not in the United States.

Catastrophism

It is curious that a well-known biologist such as John W. Kimball can author a superb biology text (*Biology, Fourth Edition;* Addison-Wesley; 1978) and yet lose his objectivity when it comes to discussing evolution. In his text he presents the following evidences of evolution, at the same time ridiculing the existence of a creator.

> *Evidence from Paleontology:* With rare exception, fossils are not remains of organisms still found on earth. A series of special creations followed by world catastrophic extinction has sometimes been given for the explanation.[1] The theory of evolution provides a more satisfactory answer, however. The idea that all organisms alive today share a common ancestry at some period in history implies that these were less complex. This describes the fossil record very well....
>
> Though we may never be able to trace the evolution of all living things through the fossils of their ancestors, the presence and distribution of fossils already discovered provide us with some of the most direct evidence of the theory of evolution. (p 576)

The student is left to ponder the unlikely series of world-wide catastrophes that "sometimes has been given for the explanation." (The straw man has struck again!) Catastrophism is usually the province of non-scientists. It is not appropriate to use such references or suppose that creationists are unscientific. The fossil record supports the sequence of creation described in Genesis as well as spontaneous evolution. In Genesis, life on earth begins with plants and animal life in the oceans, birds, animals on land, and finally humans. Perhaps the author of the biology text has never read the Bible.

> *Evidence from Comparative Anatomy:* One could argue that there was only one best way to construct the organ in question and that the Creator used it. However...if all species have

---

[1] Similarly, we read in another text: *"If an investigator studied the fossils in one rock layer and then studied the fossils in a slightly more recent layer, he would often find that those in the more recent layer, though very similar to the older ones, showed slight differences....The notion of catastrophic extinction and repeated creations hardly seemed adequate to explain such fossil sequences."* William T. Keeton, *Biological Science,* W.W. Norton & Co., 1980. Again the instructors impose catastrophic methods upon God and creationists students (who sit in embarrassed silence to the charges).

been specifically created, it seems like poor designing to include nonfunctional parts. If, on the other hand, we assume that both snakes and whales have evolved from four-legged ancestors, then we can understand why traces of their evolutionary heritage still remain. (p. 579)

Vestigial Organs

Again the author, apparently knowing how God and his agents operate, insist that he use a special creation pattern for each species and then create them by saying the word. It is not allowed that God, or one of his agents, would modify an existing pattern in a similar creature if it produced a vestigial organ in a new genus of animals. It would be acceptable to go from snakes to four-legged reptiles but not vise-versa. (We will see later in Chapter 6 why it is likely that the creation of new life forms was done by the modification of existing forms.)

This is like telling a computer programmer that he must start from scratch in developing a record-keeping program in botany rather than modify an existing record-keeping program used in zoology. It is true that a botany program made from scratch may use less memory, but programmers do not usually worry about including a few extra statements from the zoology program. Besides, they may prove useful later on.

At one time doctors thought that the thymus gland was a vestigial organ, not only of no use but detrimental to a growing child. Therefore it became a common practice to have the thymus glands of children reduced in size by x-ray treatment. Besides the thyroid cancer that developed in many of these children when they became adults, it is now known that the thymus gland is important in our resistance to disease.

It is rather officious for a scientist to say that an organ is vestigial because he has not yet found a use for it. Vestigial organs may exist, but it is more accurate to say "No use has been found for the appendix", rather than "The appendix is a vestigial organ". Biology teachers frequently support their concept of evolution by pointing out vestigial organs because they do not see vestigial organs ever being produced by an intelligent creator. The word vestigial implies that evolution has dispensed with certain organs that are no longer functional, an operation obviously not under intelligent control. The previous chapter suggested that mutation and genetic engineering are involved in evolution. Each allow for vestigial organs.

Embryology

> *Evidence from Embryology:* The temporary possession of a tail and a two-chambered heart are other examples of development stages through which the human embryo passes. Surely there must be more direct ways [for God] to achieve the final adult form.(p.580)

One of the first organs to function in an embryo is its heart. It must pump blood in order to grow more than a few cells thick, so that food and oxygen can get to the inner cells. How does the author propose that a embryo develop a four-chambered heart all at once without blood circulating so that it can develop? The logical sequence is to develop a simple two-chambered heart a few cells thick that can utilize food and oxygen by absorption, then begin to pump blood and develop into a large, more efficient, four-chambered heart. If there surely must be a more direct way to achieve a four-chambered heart, perhaps the author could suggest one. (One must wonder what the author was doing during his undergraduate course in vertebrate embryology.)

In vertebrates, the spinal column must develop before legs, since nerves control the embryological development of limbs. If you cut the nerves, the limbs stop growing. There must be a time when the spinal column extends below the leg buds in order to form the pelvic girdle. The tail mentioned is just the tail end of the spinal column, which also has a head end. Perhaps the author could also explain how an embryo's spinal column could develop without having a tail end.

In normal individuals, the end segments of the spinal column fuse to form the coccyx. This seems to be a very effective way to create a resilient "tail bone." A solid coccyx would be a disaster and a solid sacrum would have difficulty developing the openings necessary for the pelvic nerves. The sacral hiatus is used as an opening through which obstetrician may make injections to ease the pain of childbearing. Occasionally an individual is born without having these bones fused— just as in spinal bifida, occasionally the spine does not completely enclose the spinal cord.

If you were Adam, would you begin from scratch to develop insects, or would you cause a few minor genetic changes in a suitable existing arthropod so that three pair of its legs would grow longer etc? Why do evolutionists not allow God or his agents such liberties?

Biochemistry

Evidence from Comparative Biochemistry: The author also uses amino acid sequences in polypeptides chains (such as in cytochrome C), to show that man and ape are closely related and that man and fish, for example, are not. Man and ape differ in cytochrome C in only one amino acid out of a chain of 112 amino acids. This, then, is further evidence of spontaneous evolution. (pp.582-85)

Enzymes not only control the biochemistry and metabolism of an adult, but also embryological development. That is, it is impossible for ape and man to develop differently from fish unless specific enzymes are produced at the proper time in the embryo. If ape and man are to be similar in their anatomy and physiology, they must have similar genes producing similar polypeptides and enzymes. Perhaps the author could suggest how one could develop two similar animals with dissimilar enzymes.

A genetic engineer would certainly alter or add only one amino acid at a time in a polypeptide chain until a functional protein was produced if he was in the process of creating an improved species of ape. The new polypeptide would not be functional until it reached a fortuitous configuration. In reality, the fortuitous configuration would be predetermined based on three-dimensional biochemistry. Genetic engineers now use little trial and error. Single polypeptides would not likely be functional, but would work in conjunction with several others, as in the case of *Aplysia* on page 71.

Only when one was thoroughly familiar with the entire genetic code would one be well enough informed to design a group of large molecules which would operate at exactly the proper time in each cell to perform a new physiological function and/or alter anatomy in a desired way. Although no evolutionist knows how to do this, fortuitous mutations are envisioned operating this way. Is pre-existent genetic engineering less probable than fortuitous mutations?

It is interesting to compare the sequence of amino acids in proteins and enzymes of plants and animals. The number and sequence of the amino acids are almost certainly related to their evolutionary development and give valuable information as to the order in which different species appeared. But these sequences are not proof that evolution was completely spontaneous.

The increase of complexity of form in plants and animals from the beginning of life on this planet to the present time is called evolution. It has been established from the paleontological record and also described in the Bible. The Bible indicates the same sequence of events in the creation of the earth as do geological and astronomical observations.

At the present time no one seems to know to what extent God used genetic mutation and assimilation to cause evolution. The special creation of each species is an unjustified concept. It seems that speciation, at least, is caused by spontaneous gene mutation. One may wonder whether evolution was due to spontaneous gene development or to celestial genetic engineering. The assumption that it was entirely one or the other is not supported by sufficient evidence and may remain that way until the end of the Millennium.

Two related animal classes may differ by well over 1,000 genes. So far, the creation of even one additional gene by chance in a macroorganism has eluded our observation. It is possible, however, for one bacterium to assimilate a gene from another or for one animal to incorporate another's gene when invaded by a retrovirus. "Bacterial resistance to antibiotics is accomplished by bacteria of different species exchanging genetic information. Viruses not only carry their own genes from cell to cell, but those of other creatures as well." (*Smithsonian*, November, 1987, p. 126.)

Those who preach that each species was the result of a special creation are well enough rebutted by evolutionists. However, there is little unemotional criticism of the evolutionists who write biology texts such as those mentioned. High school and university biology students are often overwhelmed by the evidence presented, since it is usually given from only one point of view. This book was therefore written to help balance the scales and to criticize certain biology text authors for not being more objective when discussing God and evolution. It is hoped that science teachers who read this may use it as an example in moderating the presentation of evolution found in most texts.

Chapter Four
THE BIBLE AS HISTORY

Historical References

At the present time, the Bible is not used as a historical reference in high schools. It is, however, cited in reference to Hebrew and Jewish theology. Some historians suggest that the heroes of the Bible were mythical. As myths, the stories of the biblical heroes might be studied. Greek mythology is a popular subject in high school. However, archaeologists, historians, and classical scholars reviewing current literature are beginning to re-evaluate their point of view in light of the ancient libraries and ruins which have been discovered since World War II such as Qumran, Nag Hammadi, & Ebla. It appears now that the Bible is as historically accurate as any other source and "What the ancients had was more established and sophisticated than much of what followed."[1]

A book titled *Bible as History* presents evidence that the events mentioned in the Bible really took place. For example, the Egyptian town Medinet-el-Faiyum, eighty miles south of Cairo, is at the end of a canal over 200 miles long which is called "Bahr Yusuf" - "Joseph's Canal." Local people say that it was the Joseph of the Bible, Pharaoh's Grand Vizier, as Arab legends describe him, who planned it.[2]

In *A Revelation in Archaeology,* Chaim Berman states,

> No one could deny that the instances in which the Bible is confirmed by archaeology are numerous. In the mid-nineteenth

---

[1] Hugh Nibley, *The Earliest Christians According to the Newly Discovered Papyri*; B.Y.U. tape #590.

[2] Werner Keller, *The Bible as History,* Wm. Morrow & Co., 1956.

century, for example, cuneiform inscriptions established that Sargon, Sennacherib, Esarhaddon the son of Omri, all of whom figure fairly prominently in the Bible, were palpable historical personages. The fortifications which Solomon is said to have built at Hazor, Meggido and Gezer (I Kings 9:15) have been uncovered; while pieces of ivory recovered from Samaria illuminate Amos' condemnation of *you who loll on beds inlaid with ivory* (Amos 6:4).

The Aramaic papyri discovered in 1907/8 at Elephantine confirmed, despite wide-spread skepticism, that Aramaic was used for state correspondence in the Persian Empire, as exemplified in Ezra 4-7.

Archeological and historical support for the *Book of Mormon* has also come to light. *The Codex Nuttal* (p. 4), of the Mixtec Indians of Oacaca in southern Mexico, shows that the God Quetzalcoatl (who many identify with Christ) died on April 6th, AD 30 and was resurrected on April 9th, AD 30. Stela 5, from Izapa Mexico, is universally recognized as a *Tree of Life* representation and that the glyph of an upper jaw bone above one of the older characters represents the name *Lehi* in Hebrew.[3]

The Discovery of Ebla

Recent discoveries, such as the clay tablets from Ebla, provide additional evidence of Biblical events. Since Ebla may not be as well known as other archeological sites, I will take some time to detail some of the discoveries made there. Ebla, discovered by Paulo Matthiae in 1967-1975, is located in Syria, about 40 miles south of Aleppo. The importance of this discovery lies in the palace archives, written on nearly 20,000 clay tablets and fragments. The records bring to light a long-lost civilization of 250,000 people which rivaled those of Egypt and Mesopotamia. The records were written in cuneiform in two languages, Sumerian and a hitherto unknown Western Semetic dialect. This language, related to Hebrew, was translated by Giovanni Pettinato.

According to archaeologist and biblical scholar, David Freedman, Pettinato found the names of Sodom and Gomorrah, along with other

---

[3] *First Nephi, The Doctrinal Foundation*, Alan K. Parrish et al., p. 134, Religious Studies Center, BYU, 1988.

cities not mentioned outside the Bible, during the translation.[4] This report gives support to the biblical account of Abraham. The idea that ruins of Sodom and Gomorrah may have been submerged beneath the southern end of the Dead Sea did not seem to be a credible explanation for the fact that their ruins have yet to be identified with certainty.[5] Therefore some considered the story of Abraham a myth. According to Freedman, the name Abram also appeared. While some suppose that this refers to the Abraham of the Bible, it may refer to an earlier man with the same name. On the other hand, perhaps the accepted chronology of the Bible is in error.

Eber

It is interesting that the king of Ebla was named Ebrium. He lived at approximately the same time that Eber would have lived, who is seen to be the father of the Hebrews. According to Chaim Bermant, "Eber ('Eber) is just the expected form for the ancestors of the Hebrews ('ibri), as is Heth (Het) for the 'ancestor' of the Hittites (hitti)."[6]

There is some similarity in the genealogy of Ebrium and that of Eber in Genesis.[7]

The Sons and Grandsons of Ebrium and Eber

Ebrium	Eber
Gir-damu	Joktan
Ilmada	Almodad
Seladu	Sheleph
Zalalu	Uzal
7 other sons	10 other sons

---

[4] Professor Freedman, Director of the Program of Studies in Religion at the University of Michigan, visited Pettinato in Syria and was told confidentially of the discovery of references to Sodom and Gomorrah as well as other Biblical names. He published this information in the *Los Angeles Times* in June 1976. See also, *Ensign*, September 1980, p. 33.

[5] The Jewish historian Josephus noted that it was possible to see the remains of ancient cities south of the Dead Sea. Salt encrusted tree stumps can still be seen in the Dead Sea. In 1924, W.F. Albright discovered the ruins of a city at Bab edn-Dhra and four others have been found. Some suggest that the ruins at Bab edn-Dhra may be Sodom, although it appears to have been destroyed four centuries before the biblical date for Abraham. This date, however, coincides with the era of the Abram reported to have been found in the Ebla archives.

[6] Chaim Bermant, *A Revelation in Archaeology*, Times Books, 1979.

[7] Giovanni Pettinato, *The Archives of Ebla*, Doubleday, (1981), p. 82. Compare with Genesis 10:25.

Gir-damu does not look at all like Joktan, but Damu is a pagan god, so Gir-damu may be a secondary name.[8]

Even though Ebrium and Eber turn out to belong to different men, the similarity in the names used in the Bible and in a city in Canaan, near where Eber must have lived, certainly adds credibility to the historicity of the Bible. Notice the similarity in the names of the grandsons, *Ilmada* and *Almodad*.

According to Pettinato, the exact pronunciation of Eblaite, and perhaps biblical names, is uncertain. Consonants such as p, b, d, and t are often confused. Cuneiform writing does not distinguish between mute p and sonant b. In Eblaite, the four pair of consonants that are frequently interchanged are r/l, b/g, k/h, and g/n. For instance, the name for firstborn, "bukaru," may also be written "bukalu."

What's in a Name?

Just as we have to refer to context, or other sources, to discover the identity of God (Jehovah or Elohim) in the Bible, perhaps the Eblaites had the same problem. Many pre-Ebrium Eblaites added il to their personal names, such as Is-ra-il or Mi-ka-il (Michael; "who is like El"). During the reign of Ebrium, in Ebla, the names Is-ra-ia or Mi-ka-ia (Micah; "who is like Ya") etc. became more popular. During the reign of Ebrium, some Eblaites worshiped a god named Ya. Perhaps it was Ebrium (Eber) who identified the God who dealt with the Prophets as Ya and names ending in *ah* were given to children to gain favor. Yahweh is a Hebrew word.

El was a personal name for God, but was also used simply as God. The name Elijah would translate "Jehovah is my God." Notice how many of the Prophets used names ending in -el (-il) or -iah. If Jeremiah appeared in Eblaite, it would be as *yrmy*, which would mean "Ya is exalted." It was common for a person to be given a new descriptive name in a different country. Daniel was known as Belteshazzar in Babylon. "Christ," a Greek name meaning "The Anointed", is equivalent to the Hebrew name "Messiah."

---

[8] It was common for pagan men to be renamed with the combined names of an animal and a god. Nimrod, for instance, has been interpreted to mean "The panther of Hadd." Jacob was renamed Israel (Let God prevail), after wrestling with a man at Penuel. (Gen. 32:28)

Ebrium's successor, IbbiSipis has the name of a pagan god "Sipis" as part of his name. This was the pagan counterpart of the Hebrew names mentioned above. The four main gates of the city were also dedicated to pagan gods. Things went downhill after the time of Ebrium. There is evidence that it was during the reign of IbbiSipis that the Eblaites were conquered by the Akkadian king Naram-Sin, a grandson or grandnephew of Sargon about 2300 BC.

The Eblaite records are also the oldest present texts with the personal name Adam. In Eblaite, Adam is written as Adamu. Besides being used as a personal name, it also means "man" in Ugaritic, a contemporary language to Eblaite.

During translation of the tablets, Pettinato came across this "hymn."

> Lord of heaven and earth:
> The earth was not, you created it,
> The light of day was not, you created it
> The morning light you had not [yet] made exist.

He then states:

> This hymn to the 'Lord of heaven and earth,' with a passage referring to the origin of the cosmos as the creation of God, contains a series of appellatives which set off divinity itself. The text speaks for itself; under the form of a litany the Eblaite theologians reveal their concept of God, Lord of heaven and earth and hence of the cosmos. God is seen as a superior being but continually present upon the earth and in daily life.
>
> At this point it becomes clear that the Eblaite was profoundly religious and believed in his own gods; indeed this hymn makes it plausible that this culture, to be sure polytheistic, was on the way to a henotheism virtually declared. Who, in fact, is the Lord of heaven and earth?. Certainly not Dagan or Rasap or Sipis, but **GOD** written in capitals.

Historical Sources

It is too bad that historians feel obligated to depict the Old Testament as having been developed later on by Moses. What were all the Prophets and Elders doing during these dynasties? It is apparently not possible that they kept written records used by Moses, because none have been found. So they assume that he borrowed Canaanite stories of the creation, poetry from the Phoenicians, Akkadian legends of a flood etc., to compose the Pentateuch. After all, these were the only available sources for historians.

But records are coming to light which tell a different story. From Hugh Nibley we read,

> An interesting passage from the Book of Jubilees [a text unknown before 1850] recounts that Joseph while living in Egypt 'remembered the Lord and the words of Abraham.' (167:39,6) Here is a clear statement that the 'words of Abraham' were handed down in written form from generation to generation, and were the subject of serious study in the family circle. The same source informs us that when Joseph died and was buried in Canaan, 'he gave all his books and the books of his fathers to Levi his son that he might preserve then and renew them for his children until this day'.[9]

In 1976 Pettinato was refused access to photographs of newly discovered tablets in fear that he might find additional evidence that the Eblaites were the ancestors of Israel. According to David Freedman, it was when Pettinato discovered the word "Israel" in the Eblaite tablets that he got in hot water with the Syrians.[10] He also stated, "Preliminary studies of the bilingual vocabularies from Ebla (previously translated by Pettinato) reveal that words are preserved with the same meanings centuries later in the book of Job, for example."[11] Both Matthiae and Pettinato have stressed (or did until 1977) that Eblaite and Hebrew belong to same branch viz. North-Western Semitic.[12] Since that time nearly all their statements seem to be pro-Syrian, aimed at being able to continue research at Ebla.

Due to this pressure from Syria, Professors Pettinato and Matthiae publish very little that relates to the Bible. Each has written a book about Ebla without mentioning Sodom or Gomorrah, or any possible

---

[9] Hugh Nibley, *Abraham in Egypt,* Deseret Book, (1981) p. 5.

[10] *A Revelation in Archeology,* Bermant & Weitzman, p. 10. *The Archives of Ebla,* Giovanni Pettanito, p. 249.

[11] *The Archives of Ebla,* p. 316.

[12] *A Revelation in Archaeology,* p. 182.

Biblical ties, in the body of their text. The Syrians fear that such references may prove favorable to the Jews. Matthiae maintains that biblical connections, such as biblical patriarchs, Sodom and Gomorrah, or Yahwe worship, are non-existent. Yet, the Ya name changes from El during Ebrium's reign and names of the grandson Almodad are clearly in the record as well as the name Israel.[13]

The Ebla tablets, and records unearthed from contemporary cities, not only support the Bible as history but give new meanings to hundreds of Hebrew words which are finding their way into new translations of the Bible.[14] Whether or not Sodom, Gomorrah or Abram are found in the Ebla tablets is only a minor point.

It is unfortunate that we see Biblical sites as political tools, local environments important only for the revelations or manifestations received, or as precursors for later 'important' civilizations. Each locale had a rich religious, political, and cultural existence. Many made original contributions to what we are today. Truth is revealed in proportion to the degree of wholeness we painstakingly unearth, but not everyone wants the truth.

Elders in Ebla

Eber is one of the Hebrew Patriarchs. If the Eblaites are closely connected with Eber, then we ought to find some mention of priesthood functions in the Eblaite records. Such, indeed is the case. To quote from Pettinato,

> When treating of the top echelons of the state, we noted the presence of the "Elders," called abbu, "fathers." Who were these Elders? In this simple question is concealed one of the many enigmas of the Eblaite state....The Elders at Ebla form a

---

[13] Paulo Matthiae, Ebla: An Empire Rediscovered, Doubleday, 1977, p. 11

[14] There are 1735 Hebrew words in the Bible that occur only once. No other parallels were available until Ugaritic discoveries in 1929 and Eblaite discoveries in 1974. A major source of the Hebrew language and people seems to clearly point to Ebla. For example, in 3000 B.C. "GA-SHUM" was the Eblaite rain month. Two thousand years later we find the Hebrews using the word "GESHEM" for rain. Another example: "KA-PA-RU" in Eblaite is the word for Cyprus, a placed of copper mines. Later we find the word "KOPER" meaning payment or bribe. Finally we find the Hebrew word "KIPPER" meaning "to reconcile" and the Jewish word "YOM KIPPUR" meaning "Day of Reconciliation with God." Ibid. Chapter Nine. Also, Archives at Ebla, pp.315-318, and Francis L. Filas, The Ebla Tablets, Loyola U. (tape & filmstrip).

kind of senate that controls the king in his exercise of power....They are not to be looked on as a superceded body but as an assembly very active and influential in most important decisions. They are mentioned together with the king, they are listed among the high positions of the state, . . . they send letters to the prince heir warning him to take care—these all demonstrate both the limitations of the king's powers and the central role of the Elders in the hierarchy of the state.[15]

The Eblaites, like the Sumerians, referred to their king as the 'vicar of God' and the political leaders were accessible to the citizens. In contrast, Mesopotamians such as the Akkadians, regarded Sargon as the 'God of Akkad' and there was a rigid separation between political powers and business of daily life.[16] If any of the Bible Patriarchs held political power, and many did, the political structure would have been along Sumerian lines.

Eblaite and Sumerian[17] tablets show that exquisite poetic and writing skill existed before 2,500 B.C. Language and writing skill seems to have suddenly appeared in all cultures about the same time, just prior to 3,000 B.C. This corresponds well with the time of the Biblical flood and is an unexplained phenomenon to the evolutionist. We find sophisticated concepts in the oldest known texts.[18]

To be sure, improvements were made to simplify writing, but languages have first appeared remarkably well developed. The 2,000 separate signs for words (ideograms) in Sumerian were reduced to 500 Eblaite syllables and consonants. Eighty percent of the Eblaite syllables and consonants are older Sumerian ideograms used phonetically. "The

---

[15] *The Archives at Ebla*, p. 93.

[16] *Ibid.* pp. 222-223.

[17] *Enmerkar and the Lord of Aratta* is a Sumerian heroic poem written around 2,000 B.C. about legendary events 1,000 years earlier when Enmerkar ruled Erech. Erech was one of Nimrod's cities (Gen.10:10). Since k & h were sometimes confused in translating cuneiform, and we replace the k in Enmerkar with h, we have Enmerhar which does have a resemblance to Nimrod. However, the point is that this poem was 600 lines long and involved power-politics suggestive of our own day. It was once written on a clay tablet only nine by nine inches in dimension, indicating a well advanced form of writing. An even longer Sumerian *Epic of Gilgamesh* (3,500 lines) exists. He also was a legendary king of Erech. See *History Begins at Sumer*, Chapters 4 & 23, Samuel Kramer, Doubleday, 1959.

[18] Hugh Nibley, *The Timely and the Timeless*, Religious Studies Center BYU (1978), p. 24.

offhand manner and mastery of Sumerian writing that permit such a practice can only represent the final or mature phase of an ancient and widespread development. At present, the oldest texts come from Uruk, where the characters are certainly not primitive."[19]

Sumerian was the cultivated language of the bureaucracy and priesthood at Ebla, just as Egyptian Hieroglyphics continued as the writing of the Pharoahs and priests of Egypt for sacred and monumental writing even up to 394 A.D. in the Temple of Isis at Philae. For example *e'dingr*, a sacred word for temple (house of God) in Eblaite, was always written in Sumerian. In Egypt, a simplified form of hieroglyphics, Hieratic, and an even more cursive form, Demotic, was used for secular purposes.

The Sumerians

Early Sumerians used pictographic writing. When writing in clay became popular, it was found better to press the edge of a stylus into the clay rather than scratch it and leave ragged edges. This became cuneiform writing. For example the characters for *ox* and *bird* in pictogram and cuneiform are written below. (Cuneiform is easier to write horizontally.)[20]

	Primitive Pictogram	Intermediate Stages	Ninevite Cuneiform
bird			
ox			

---

[19] *The Archives at Ebla*, p. 265.

[20] *A Revelation in Archaeology*, p. 118.

Some Ugaritic cuneiform alphabetic letters

Sign	Equivalent	Sign	Equivalent	Sign	Equivalent
▷–	'a		'i		'u
𒁹	b		g		d
▷–	k		l		m
⊨	p		q		r
⋈	t		w		z

According to Chaim Bermant, "The name 'Sumer' is more properly 'Shumer' and leaving off the final consonant, as the city Ur is called Urim in the Bible, we end with Shume which may have entered the Bible as Shem."[21] It is interesting that "All attempts to relate Sumerian to other known languages have failed." Why this is interesting is that, according to the Bible, it was after Shem that the languages were confounded. Is it possible that in the study of ancient Sumerian we encounter a somewhat corrupted form of the Adamic language?

Mitchell Dahood of Rome's Pontifical Biblical Institute says, "After Ebla, we've got to take the Bible much more seriously as a historical document."[22] These documents are causing churches to re-examine their doctrine and ordinances. Perhaps they may cause evolutionists to wonder if the Biblical account of the creation, God's existence, and his dealings with man may also have some validity.

---

[21] *Time Magazine*, Sept. 21, 1981, p. 77.
[22] *Ibid.*

Chapter Five
IN THE BEGINNING

The First Period of Creation

Let us examine the account of the creation, as given in the first verses of Genesis, and see if there is any agreement between it and present scientific thinking.

> In the beginning God created the heaven and the earth (Gen. 1:1).

(This is described in more detail by Abraham in the *Pearl of Great Price.* "We will go down, for there is space there, and we will take of these materials, and we will make an earth wherein these may dwell" [Abr.3:24]).

Scientists envision the creation of the solar system as a condensation of dust and gas in a small section of the Milky Way. This condensation is seen to be accomplished by gravity over a period of thirty million to one hundred million years. Using laws of physics, such a condensation of gas and dust was recently studied with the aid of a computer.[1] The computations show that certain aggregations of particles will indeed form a solar system through mutual gravitational attraction. These computer-generated solar systems sometimes contain two or more suns, and indeed multiple star systems have been observed within our galaxy. However, only single-sun solar systems are ideal for life on one of the planets. The temperature extremes on the inner planets would be excessive in solar systems with two or more suns.

We see by astronomical observations and by computer simulation that the earth was probably not created in one day or a few thousand

---

[1] *Scientific American*, June, 1981.

years. Even if God could have created the earth in six days, it is unlikely that he would do so. It would require a vast amount of time to give God's 150,000,000,000 spirit children sufficient time to gain practical experience in this creative process. (There will have been an estimated 100 billion people on the earth by the end of the Millennium—circa 3,000 A.D.)

> And the earth was without form and void; and darkness was upon the face of the deep (Gen. 1:2).

It was only after most of the gas forming the sun was collected and compressed by gravity that it was able to create light by electromagnetic reactions. Up to that time the earth was a dark cloud of gas and dust and void of life. Even the light of the stars was obscured within the local pockets of collecting gas and dust.

> And the spirit of God moved upon the face of the waters (Gen. 1:2).

At this point, in the formation of the solar system, nothing was solid.

> And God said, Let there be light: and there was light (Gen. 1:3).

Visible light was first produced by the sun by electromagnetic interactions due to gravitational collapse. When the core of the sun reached thirty million degrees, it began producing light by thermonuclear reactions. At that temperature the sun's hydrogen began fusing into helium releasing energy, a process that creates the sun's energy today, and will continue to do so for at least ten billion years.

> And God saw the light, that is was good (Gen.1:4).

Stars produce infra-red, visible, and ultra-violet light as well as showering us with atomic particles called cosmic rays. Some of the ultra-violet light and cosmic rays are so strong that they can destroy all forms of life, even millions of miles away. If there is an atmosphere of air to cover the earth, the cosmic and ultraviolet rays will be absorbed and converted into less energetic radiant energy which is generally beneficial to plants and animals. These cosmic and ultra-violet rays are the forces scientists suppose supplied the energy necessary to form proteins from the oceanic mineral solutions.

But this cosmic energy will destroy protein molecules as rapidly as they are formed. Therefore there must be a proper level of radiation for spontaneous protein synthesis to be accomplished (if such a thing is possible) and the simple proteins must be removed to an area where there is less thermal and radiant energy if they are to combine properly into larger molecules. We are presently protected from ultra-violet rays by an ozone layer, which is composed of oxygen atoms. This protection may not have been available from the earth's primitive atmosphere since plants were not yet in existence to produce the necessary levels of oxygen. However, at a time, when the average temperature of the ocean was about 100°F, replicating proteins may have been formed.

This would have been the optimum time for life to begin spontaneously if it was ever going to happen. At a certain point, God must have instructed Christ and Adam to begin one-celled life from the molecules that had been spontaneously developed or to transplant cells from a prior planet. Although remotely possible, it is unlikely that the necessary one-celled plants developed spontaneously.

Temperatures above 100°F cause too much thermal agitation to allow development of DNA-type molecules due to the delicate organic bonds. This is one reason why temperatures of 110°F are dangerous to animals. Another reason is that metabolism increases with temperature. A 10°F increase would cause body cells to increase their metabolism and heart rate by 50%. Temperatures below 90°F do not provide enough thermal energy for rapid organic chemical reactions. This is why cold-blooded animals are inert or tire more easily than warm-blooded animals when the ambient temperature is low. Snakes and lizards have low metabolism which stores energy slowly. When they are warmed by the sun they metabolize and restore ATP energy more rapidly.[2] Warm blooded animals have a higher metabolism rate, storing and releasing energy quickly. They require more food and oxygen than cold-blooded animals in order to maintain their 100°F temperature.[3]

---

[2] ATP is adenosine triphosphate. It is the chief source of quick energy in all animals, including man. It is created by the metabolism of glucose or other sugars.

[3] Our internal temperature is about one degree higher than when taken sublingually. About one-third of our food energy is used to maintain our tropical internal temper ature. Cold-blooded animals need little food energy to keep them alive when they are cold.

It is speculated that at this time the ocean water was about 1% salt, and represents the salt concentration of the blood in all animals today. Thus the spontaneous development of life did not have billions of years to be accomplished but had to happen in a fairly narrow time slot when conditions were just right.

To create orderly structures the laws of thermodynamics have to be satisfied. In order to build up one system, you must borrow energy from another system. The natural order of things is to go from order to disorder. This is called entropy and follows from the Second Law of Thermodynamics. To build a DNA chain from simple molecules, with only thermal energy to guide it, is a difficult problem that has yet to be solved.

To build an organic molecule, man must control the chemical concentrations and the energy flow of the reactants in dozens of precise sequential steps. You must ask the question, "Is it more likely that an intelligent being created life, or chance?" You must consider the capability man now has and that there ought to be other worlds where intelligent life has progressed far beyond ours. But, if intelligent beings created life on this earth, where are they now? We do not see them! The term "we do not see them", is in reality, "most do not see them", because there are also many, including the author, who know that they exist. (See page 112.) The president of a large corporation only allows his receptionist to admit to his presence those he desires to see.

> And God divided the light from the darkness (Gen. 1:4).

When one is in a fog, it is hard to say whether one is in the light or in darkness. The same is true of the gas and dust that collected to form the earth and planets. Only when the earth was solid and rotating could one say that there was definite light and darkness.

> And God called the light Day, and the darkness Night. And the evening and the morning were the first day. (Gen. 1:5)

We are now discussing a solid earth which is rotating.

The Second Period of Creation

> And God said, Let there be a firmament in the midst of the waters, and let it divide the waters from the waters (Gen 1:6).

And God made the firmament, and divided the (great) waters which were under the firmament from the waters which were above the firmament: And it was so (Gen. 1:7).

And God called the firmament Heaven. And the evening and the morning were the second day (Gen. 1:8).

Just as physicists use the term fluids to describe liquids or gases, the word waters in the Bible may also indicate liquids or gases. That this may be so is indicated by the fact that 'waters' is plural, indicating variety. The Pearl of Great Price (Moses 2:7) tells us that the waters under the firmament were more massive than the waters above the firmament, a condition we see today. The water vapor in the air is less than 0.01% of the water in the ocean. The flood of Noah could not have come from rain alone. How did Moses know that? How did he know that the water in the earth's crust would be needed to accomplish this deluge (Gen. 7:11)?

One might use the following analogy to describe the formation of the solar system. "Suppose you take an eraser covered with chalk dust and spread the chalk dust over a blackboard. This then represents the dust and gas in a section of the Milky Way before it became the solar system. Now take a clean eraser and erase an oval area in the middle of the chalkboard. Remove most of the chalk accumulated on the clean eraser with your finger and place it in the middle of the oval. This represents the sun. Now take smaller amounts of chalk remaining on the eraser and make a few planets. This not only demonstrates the collecting of gas and dust to form the solar system but demonstrates that the space between the planets is relatively free from space dust."

Just as the condensation of the sun produced great heat to ignite its nuclear furnace, so also the condensation of the material forming the earth, along with the radioactive decay of atoms within the earth, produced heat. While the earth's crust was near the boiling point of water, there would have been a dense cloud of water vapor covering the entire earth, perhaps 100 miles deep. At that time, the surface of the earth would be completely dark, and life would not be possible.

As the earth cooled, it became possible for water to remain longer on the earth's crust and for the humidity of the air to fall below 100%. A clearing (firmament or heaven) would then appear between the surface of the ocean and the clouds above.

And God said, Let the waters under the heaven be gathered into one place and let dry land appear. And it was so (Gen. 1:9).

The Miracle of Continents

Why we have continents is nothing short of miraculous—no other planets have them. Only very careful planning or exact accidental combinations of temperature, mineral composition and internal geologic structure could have produced them. Otherwise the earth would have remained completely covered by water except for volcanic islands. The earth's crust might have been a layer of granitic rock several miles thick covered by a world ocean two miles deep. This is a natural consequence of less dense materials forming on top of denser materials. The layer of rock beneath the oceans and granitic continents is called basalt and is 10% more dense than granite. There is no granite covering the ocean basins.

Buoyancy calculations show that it would take a continental depth of twenty miles for granitic continents to float above basalt to the present height of two and one-half miles. This made it possible for the primeval world ocean, which must have been slightly less than two miles deep, to drain off the granite continents and fill the basalt basins, forming oceans more than two miles deep.

Large continents have been created for terrestrial plants and animals. George Gamow believed that the continents were formed when the moon was created from the crust and underlying material from the Pacific Ocean area.[4] This is an incredible idea, but it is well known that

---

[4] George Gamow, *Biography of the Earth*, Mentor #138. Our moon is unusually large. No other planet has a moon one-fourth of its own diameter. An average-size moon would give little light to the Earth by the reflection of sunlight. (Another fortunate accident.)

At a time when the earth was spinning more rapidly, its rotation not only required more centripetal force to hold the earth's crust, but tidal action due to the sun's gravity may have caused severe oscillations, like the Washington Narrows bridge, as its period of rotation and natural frequency of oscillation coincided.

According to George Gamow, this oscillation of the outer surface around a massive core made it possible for a piece of the earth to be separated and drift into space. Since the mantle was quite plastic the piece that left reformed into a sphere. The density of the moon is quite low and is consistent with mantle and crust material, and the minerals found in moon rocks are very similar to earth rocks (See *Scientific American*, Aug. 1970, p. 14.) This theory has been recently revised with the addition of a meteorite collision to fill the role of mid-wife. *Space Time Infinity*, James S. Trefil, Smithsonian Books, 1985, p. 158 and *Discover*, March 1985, p. 64.

This theory of the moon's origin also provides the continental crust exposure for the Earth.

the moon has slowly drifted away from the earth. An alternate, and more modern, explanation is that continental granite was created in subduction zones in the earth's crust and eventually collected to form continents.[5]

Remarkable Accidents

It was fortunate that the ocean basins were filled with just the right amount of water, with a little left over to wash over the edges of the continents. This allowed shallow fresh water seas to form,[6] enabling the earth to be blessed later with coal and oil. To evolutionists, this was just one of a series of remarkable accidents that made this world liveable for man, just as was either the disappearance of 70% of the earth's crust or the generation of the present continents.

But this planet is more than just liveable. It is hard to conceive how to make it more suitable or beautiful. If there were less gravitational attraction, there would not be enough friction for rapid movement. If there were more gravity, it would require too much energy to move around. If the earth were tilted more or less, the needed seasonal changes would be too great or too small. If we were closer to or farther from the sun, we would be too hot or too cold. If the oceans were larger or smaller, we wouldn't have enough land or precipitation. If the earth's mountain ranges were parallel to the prevailing winds, rather than perpendicular to them, we would be constantly facing hurricane force winds and there would be little snow in the mountains for Summer water.

The list of fortunate accidents goes on and on. To many scientists, however, this list of fortunate accidents must occur occasionally in a universe containing countless billions of solar systems. We are just one of the lucky few.

---

[5] John J. Merrill, *Physical Science Fundamentals*, p. 269. Burgess Pub. Co., 1982. This should require the granite near the center of continental plates to be older and some what different from marginal granite. The continent's uniform thickness is not well explained.

[6] The most recent fresh water sea existed as recently as two thousand years ago, when central Brazil was a shallow fresh-water sea draining southward over Argentina. South America was a long narrow mountain land except for a large island where the eastern Brazilian highlands now are. The Amazon River came into existence when there was a slight continental uplift and the drainage forced its way through the highlands.

It may be less well known, but the odds that the universe was created by accident is seen to be an even more unlikely event. Below is a paragraph from The Inflationary Universe, by Paul Davies.[7]

> The rate of cosmic expansion presents still another puzzle. If the universe has been decelerating ever since it first went bang, then, if the bang had been less violent, the cumulative gravity of all the cosmic material would long since have caused the entire universe to fall back on itself. Alternatively, had the bang been more violent, the cosmos would have dispersed so quickly that galaxies would have never formed and the density of matter would now be minute. For some mysterious reason, the vigor of the explosion was matched so delicately to the gravitating power of the universe that the galaxies had just enough speed to escape each other's gravity, yet not so much as to rapidly disperse.
>
> The universe seems to lie precisely on the borderline between the alternatives of too much gravity and too much violence. It is fascinating to compute how finely tuned this cosmic balancing act had to be. The matching of explosive vigor to gravitating power was accurate to no less than one part in 10^{60}. This astonishing fidelity has perplexed cosmologists for a long time. Why should the universe be arranged to such phenomenal accuracy? Was it by some cosmically beneficent coincidence?

To overcome the improbability of the existence of our organized universe, some scientists suggest, "The universe spends the overwhelming majority of its time in total chaos, with no organization whatsoever. But, from time to time, after intervals of mind-bending duration, there occurs a few billion years of accidental order. The reason we—humanity—are present to witness one such occurrence of staggering improbability is simply because, in the absence of such a miracle, life could not exist."[8] In rebuttal, Paul Davies counters, "But, from their own reasoning, life would more likely exist in a universe with one solar system or one galaxy. Our universe is still very, very highly improbable."[9]

---

[7] Paul Davies, *The Sciences*, Mar.-Apr. 1983, p. 33.

[8] Paul Davies, *God and the New Physics*, p. 168.

[9] *Ibid*, p. 174.

Other Earths

It is easier to calculate the number of stars in our own galaxy than to count them. Newton's and Kepler's laws show that the mass (M) within the orbit of a satellite equals

$$M = 39.5 \ R^3/GT^2$$

If we know the radius (R) of the sun's orbit around the Milky Way Galaxy, the time (T) it takes for one revolution, and the gravitational constant (G), we can calculate the mass of the material in the galaxy within the sun's orbit. We then divide this mass by the mass of an average sun, such as our sun. This gives the approximate number of suns within our orbit of the Milky Way Galaxy, 100 billion. The assumption is that most of this mass has been converted into star systems, which of course is not true, but this error is offset by the number of Milky Way stars outside our galactic orbit.

Astronomer Howard Shapley estimated that there are one hundred trillion solar systems in the universe. He predicted that one of every trillion had a planet like the Earth's. This leaves one hundred million planets like the Earth in the universe if his estimation is correct.

More recent estimations indicate that 50% of the 10^{22} plus stars in the universe have solar systems with planets, allowing 10 billion earth-like planets to exist. The next question we must ask is are the earth-like planets in the proper stage of development for life with intelligence equal or greater than our own to exist. A few who contemplate the improbability of the spontaneous, accidental beginning of life have concluded that we are the only planet with such life in the universe. Others, such as Carl Sagan, estimate that there are upwards of 100,000 planets with such intelligence in our Milky Way galaxy alone. But LDS people do not have to wonder about extra-terrestrial life. In the *Pearl of Great Price* we read, "And worlds without number have I created." Also, "There are many worlds that have passed away by the word of my power. And there are many that now stand." (Moses 4: 33, 35)

Since many stars were created billions of years before our sun, it stands to reason that we are not the first humans to inhabit a planet. A fairly in-depth study of anatomy should lead one to conclude that humans have a nearly optimum structure for maximum development. Some may disagree, but have a hard time detailing any improvements. If we could visit another planet that had gone through the same industrial revolution, we would probably be unable to tell that we were not on earth, except that the animals, plants, constellations and language would be different. Even their tools and mechanical devices would be similar to ours.

Life on Other Earths

Only if life began in a different environment would life forms be different. Biologists say that the reason we find the present environment so suitable and pleasant is that we naturally fit into the environment that produced us. But one must wonder why nearly all fresh and salt water animals have the same internal environment, none having developed independently, when the ocean had a different salinity, or when things were hotter. One could argue that late-comers would have all been eaten by the more advanced 1% animals. That still leaves the absence of the 1/2% animals, which obviously did not develop. Conditions must have not become favorable until the ocean was 1% salt.

Considering the fairly narrow time slot for the development of life, one may conclude that 1% animals probably occur wherever there is life—in other words, just like ours. This does not preclude the development of many plants and animals that we would be totally unfamiliar with. If Adam came from another planet, it would seem that all planetary people are of the same race.

One may ask if the same DNA biology would have developed without the earth producing coal, oil, and nuclear reserves. The answer is very likely. The fact that we have them is pure luck according to evolutionists. Would the same biology have developed if the earth were a little nearer or farther from the sun? Again, the answer is, very likely. The flora and fauna would simply have developed nearer the poles or equator. The fact that the temperate zone is between the equator and the poles, giving the greatest use of the earth to its living creatures, is just another fortunate accident. These are improbables that have little to do with the concept "I am here, therefore the spontaneous creation of the Universe and earth life must have taken place, however improbable."

Science is supposed to be statistically plausible. The plethora of fortunate accidents that produced our present world would represent an extreme deviation from what ought to be found here. It seems that the normal curve applies to all scientific disciplines except evolution.

One question Einstein pondered was, "Could God have produced a different set of atoms in creating the Universe?" Spectroscopic analysis of the stars shows that the universe is made of the same kinds of atoms. Research also shows that anti-matter worlds are not likely to exist.[10] It appears that life anywhere must be based on the carbon atom and must follow our same laws of biochemistry. Biochemistry shows that the bonds between organic molecules in living things are very delicate and must be formed and broken by specially built enzymes, all of which must take place within a very narrow temperature range. This is why heat can produce death and mutations. The enzymes that open the intricate bonds between the nucleotides in a DNA chain must be able to do so with a very, very small expenditure of energy—which could not be easily controlled at higher or lower temperatures. Thus, the body temperatures of living things on other planets would be like on earth.

The only other chemistry that will allow the same kind of complex molecule building is silicon. This chemistry would have to take place at a much higher temperature, making the bonding of complex molecules very difficult if not impossible to control by silicon-based 'enzymes.' The conlusions one must reach are that life throughout the universe is similar, and creatures from one world would probably be able to live very well on any other planet with life. The exception would be if the biochemistry of life on another planet was based on d-amino acids. Life here is based on l-amino acids and somewhat on d-sugars.

Spontaneous Life

To demonstrate that life could have developed spontaneously, evolutionists cite the Urey and Miller experiment in which organic molecules were produced from a mixture of sparked gases representing the gases and electrical storms in our primitive atmosphere. This experiment was done in 1953 and has been repeated with similar results, none of which lead to a scenario for creating the simplest form of life. A process that could happen spontaneously in nature ought to be discoverable and reproducible.

---

[10] Murray Gell-Man lecture, University of Utah, 1983.

The 1953 experiment is still referred to because the latest experiments have yet to show something new, except a more complete identification of the amino acids that are produced. In more recent experiments, a greater variety and complexity of organic molecules were produced by careful control of the raw materials and reactants. In living organisms, amino acids combine to form peptides which can combine to form proteins, but proteins and DNA chains are not formed in the experiments. Even in cells, if mRNA genes are not immediately protected, they will quickly disintegrate into their constituent parts before ever reaching the ribosomes.

Adam's Rib

If such a spontaneous development of living organisms is demonstrated to be possible, the remoteness of the possibility for life to begin that way will also be demonstrated. The story of Eve being created from Adam's rib may be symbolic of God's first creation, or the creation of the sexes, as well as referring directly to Adam and Eve. The first living organisms on the earth were asexual. Additional comments on Adam's rib are found in the Epilogue. But for now, answer this question: "Do you believe that Adam could have demonstrated a missing rib to Abel?" One may interject; "I don't really care if Adam had a missing rib!" If that is the answer, it must also be supposed that one doesn't care about God's use of symbolism with all the discoveries and relationships it can unfold.

Do you see any agreement between the sequence of events outlined in the Bible and the detailed account of scientists? The biblical account was written by Moses about 1,500 B.C. Science had its beginnings 1000 years later. The creation of the earth was not discussed by scientists until the Eighteenth Century. What is the explanation for this agreement? How could Moses have known that the surface of the earth was one completely covered by water and the water collected into one place, and all the continental mass was in one piece (which geologists call Pangaea)? If geologists cite colleagues Suess and Taylor for the concept of a supercontinent, then why not cite Moses, the most original source?

In reading the first ten verses of Genesis about the order of creation, we find that Moses had a good batting average according to the order as seen by science. Moses condensed the whole sequence of evolution in laymans language into one short chapter. Perhaps evolutionists should try to do the same before being critical of his lack of detail. If statistics mean anything, Genesis chapter one ought to be extremely relevant. Yet, the statistics evolutionists presently accept are that we exist in a universe which has an organization so perfect that one would expect it to occur in one out of 10^{60} randomly produced universes.

I suspect, however, that it will be found that gravitational force and big-bang explosive energy are always as perfectly matched as they they are in our universe, regardless of the amount of big-bang material in the initial explosion. This would negate these extreme odds to some extent. Still, if one considers the number of fortunate accidents mentioned, and assumes that each one occurs in one out of ten planets, it would take only six such fortunate accidents to make the likelyhood of our world so well prepared for humans one out of 10^6, or one in a million.

Chapter Six
INSTINCT

Why do birds migrate? The most obvious reason is to obtain food all year round. Yet a bobolink born in early summer, and never having seen winter, will migrate to South America while it is still hot and insects are still plentiful. It returns to nest in March or April. Birds usually follow certain flyways when migrating.

It has been found that birds of many species will migrate independently of adult birds, setting out on a course they have apparently never before traveled. Research has shown that many of these birds use pole stars to orient their course.[1]

Some scientists have proposed that the birds possessed a genetically inherited star map. Scientists who discredit this idea have yet to come up with something better.

Upon returning to a hive, bees do one of two dances, which tell other bees how far away a food source is and where it is in relation to the sun. When the food source is in the same direction as the sun, the bee performs the straight portion of the wagging dance vertically, with the head pointing upward. If the food source is at some angle to the right or left of the sun, the scout bee does the straight portion of the dance at the same angle from the vertical.[2]

A worker bee goes out after pollen, following those instructions, ten days after she is born.

---

[1] *Scientific American,* August, 1975.

[2] John W. Kimball, *Biology,* Fourth Edition, Addison-Wesley, 1978, p. 538.

Genetically Controlled Behavior

Only the simple behavior aspect of instinct is fairly well understood. Simple behaviors have been shown to be inherited. For example, two types of lovebirds, which build nests differently, when crossed, will produce offspring that will try to build the nest both ways at the same time and become completely frustrated. Numerous genetically controlled simple behavior patterns are very well documented. Experiments transferring genetic material from one bacterium to a different type have shown that behavior is also transferred. Thus, many animals inherit simple behavior patterns according to the laws of heredity.

The egg-laying behavior of a marine snail, *Aplysia*, has been carefully studied by Richard H. Sheller, Richard Axel, and others. The injection of an egg-laying hormone into an unmated snail causes it to expel a string of eggs, grasp the string with its mouth, entangle the string, and affix the tangled egg string to a solid object.

This behavior is shown to be initiated by genetic control. Specific genes produce a series of peptides which act as neurotransmitters, neuroinhibitors, and as neurohormones.[3] At least seven separate peptides, which act on specific neurons, have been identified. These are produced by three genes from a polypeptide they each produce. The peptides contain 5 to 36 amino acids. If the seven peptides necessary for this operation were a chance event, how likely is it that they would be produced in series on the same genes? This is the way an intelligent creator would do it. Random evolution basically requires one gene for each protein.

The three polypeptides produced by the genes also contain several other peptides which have unknown functions. It is assumed by evolutionists that they are non-functioning spare peptides which may mutate and, in combination with other peptides produced elsewhere, create another evolutionary step or a different behavior pattern that may be beneficial to survival. Notice that this evolutionary scenario suggests the other peptides produced just wait around until they can fortuitously combine with still other peptides to perform some advanced

---

[3] Neurotransmitters are chemicals such as adrenalin which transfer nerve impulses across a synapse, a place where two nerves make contact. Neuroinhibitors, such as GABA, make it more difficult for neurotransmitters to initiate a response in the target neuron. Other chemicals are needed to deactivate and remove neurotransmitters and neuroinhibitors from the synaptic gap.

function which is the antithesis of what happened to initiate the egg-laying behavior.

The egg-laying genes are thought of as having been created about the same time. "The gene encoding the largest peptide apparently triplicated in turn, giving rise to three independent genes that diverged as they became specialized to satisfy different functional requirements."[4] The indication that all three egg-laying genes were created at the same time by triplication is evidence of intelligent creation. The bow and arrow method was not used. Unless the genes know what will enhance their survivability, which is the 'summum bonum' of the biological evolutionists, all these specialized developments are seen as simply fortuitous. Their only other explanation is that genes possess more intelligence than the creatures they create!

Why Evolution?

Where did we come from, why are we here, and where are we going? These are important questions which LDS theology answers with concepts that motivate and inspire. For a long time the evolutionists had no answer to such questions, but the questions were too persistent to ignore. There must be an answer to the question, Why? The evolutionists are now breathing easier. They have discovered why evolution has taken place. The reason for our existence is to perpetuate genes! We exist as machines to help genes survive. How motivating! How inspirational! If needs for belonging, recognition, and achievement are produced genetically, why are they unfulfilled by the concept 'we exist to serve our genes?" Let us read from a recent book on this subject.

> Why do even enormous animals and plants like elephants and sequoias go through the huge bother of rebuilding an entire organism from a single cell for each generation? The answer to this question has been most clearly expressed (by) R. Dawkins and W.D. Hamilton. It is the gene that is the important object as far as natural selection is concerned. The other materials are to give them an environment in which they can flourish.
>
> Under some environmental circumstances the genes have a good chance of survival if they are carried by large organisms. These

---

[4] *Scientific American*, Mar. 1984, p. 61.

large organisms become an efficient survival machine for perpetuating and protecting the genes. (*The Evolution of Culture in Animals*, John Bonner, Princeton University Press, 1980.)

The egg-laying genes of *Aplysia* must produce many peptides which activate or deactivate neurons that did not exist until genes produced them. These neurons have to be 'hard wired' in certain positions, attaching to specific muscle fibers and other neurons.

As you can see, it takes intricate preparation to initiate a simple behavior. The genetic development that initiated this behavior is so elegant that one must wonder how three genes could have been accidentally created about the same time to accomplish this feat. All this, according to the evolutionists, is to evolve a higher form which will provide a better survival machine for the genes. According to evolutionists, some genes must mutate in order to do this. But does a gene survive if it mutates?

A Well Planned Operation

What has been described in this study of *Aplysia* does not look at all like a chance occurrence. It looks like a well planned operation produced by a superior intellect. And what an exciting project! Designing genes which would produce the necessary neurons and peptides that would initiate such behavior looks just like the sort of thing God's spirit children ought to be learning.

We become like God (the goal He persistently and generously places before us), not only by our loyalty to God and charitable acts, but by our intellectual achievements. There is no question in the author's mind that we spent many satisfying hours on such projects in the spirit world. We evolved flora and fauna when the advances needed did not take place by natural selection.[5]

Few religions discuss what we may be doing after we die. Yet members of these same religions seem appalled at the idea that man might become like God and be involved in doing the works of the one whom we call Father. How presumptuous to imagine that we could be involved in creation or judgment. Shakespeare did not share this

---

[5] An optimized mutation rate for natural selection on the earth would be largely controlled by the proper level of background radiation.

restricted opinion. On man, he writes, "How noble in reason! How infinite in faculty! In form and moving, how express and admirable! In action, how like an angel! In apprehension, how like a God."

Most educators are familiar with Bloom's taxonomy of cognative hierarchies. A brief summary is made below:[6]

1. *Knowledge.* Knowledge is the remembering of previously learned material. Knowledge represents the lowest level of learning.

2. *Comprehension.* Comprehension is the ability to grasp the meaning of material. This represents the lowest level of understanding.

3. *Application.* Application is the ability to use learned material in new and concrete situations.

4. *Analysis.* Analysis is the ability to break down material into its component parts so that its organizational structure may be understood.

5. *Synthesis.* Synthesis is the ability to put parts together to form a new whole. This stresses creative behavior.

6. *Evaluation.* Evaluation is concerned with the ability to judge based on definite criteria.

How is it that some would deny the use of synthesis and evaluation in heaven, the two highest levels of cognative behavior? Notice how Bloom describes synthesis as creativity. Are we encouraged to create on earth, only to be denied that joy in heaven and be required to regress to behavior limited to knowledge and comprehension?

Perhaps we can create if we don't go too far. But God puts no upper limits on our hopes and dreams. If we dream of correcting genetic defects and rehabilitating the fallen here on earth, of what shall we dream in heaven? If our ultimate joy is now our children, what will our ultimate joy be then? There will be times when we will extend the fullness of our love to the Lord through praise and adoration, but some religions cannot comprehend what else we might be doing. Our

---

[6] Teachers in church settings should analyze their lesson presentations and consider the limits they make upon the learning of class members. Are the questions and discussions relegated to the lower levels of knowledge and comprehension with a brief comment on application reserved to complete the lesson? Such a level may be insulting to the intelligence of the class. Parables focus on application. Prophesies and allegories such as the tree of life and and the olive tree require thoughtful analysis, synthesis and evaluation.

love for the Lord will continuously be demonstrated as we keep his covenants.

Mini-Creations

Would God or Christ want to create anything if they already knew how? Did Adam do it all under their direction? Adam, in one of the most ancient languages known, Ugaritic, means 'man.' We should be familiar with the idea that when God gives commandments or makes covenants with Adam, they also apply to us. Would not the creation assignment also apply?

These mini-creations were under the direction of Adam,[7] who answered to Christ, who answered to God. They were much more enlightening and challenging than harp playing. The transportation of advanced forms from another planet (perhaps used as a back-up system in case our efforts proved unsatisfactory) would be a rare event.

---

[7] According to some interpretations, at one time Brigham Young advanced the idea that Adam was the father of our spirits. This idea comes mostly from a sermon on April 9, 1852 in which he states; "Jesus, our Elder Brother, was begotten in the flesh by the same character that was in the Garden of Eden, and who is our Father in heaven." Many church authorities say that the only correct interpretation of this statement is that Brigham Young is referring to, and identifies, the father of Jesus Christ as our Father in heaven. God talked to Adam in the Garden of Eden. A good commentary on this is found in *Evidences and Reconciliations,* John A. Widtsoe, p. 68.)

Although we know very little about God, and even though we are told that it is life eternal to know God, (not just his commandments), we hesitate to rock the boat of traditional concepts. Is it prudent to ask if there is the slightest chance that Brigham Young did believe that Adam was the father of some of our spirits? Should we ponder this possibility even though it seems that Christ is spiritually superior to Adam since it is to Christ that Adam will deliver up his stewardship at Adam-ondi-Ahman?

If one found out that Adam was referred to as "The Ancient of Days," is a God in Heaven, is the one with whom we dealt with in the creation, is the father of the human race, and had perhaps other information, it is not hard to see why someone, even a Prophet, could conceive of this idea. Prophets also learn line upon line and test theories.

In both the *Testament* and *Apocalypse of Abraham,* "Abraham is given an instructional tour of the universe, but also spends most of the time among the hosts of the dead....His compassion for the dead is shared, and surpassed, by that of the glorious man on the throne, the judge, who is none other than Adam, the parent of them all...who is decked out in glory...as the wicked or the righteous pass before him." (*Abraham in Egypt,* Hugh Nibley, p. 29.) One can imagine how impressed Abraham was with Adam's position after viewing such a scene.

What the author gets from Brigham Young's discourses is that Adam will be and is a God to us, and many of our future dealings will be with Adam.

The Day of Rest?

"And on the seventh day God ended his work which he had made; and he rested on the seventh day from all his work which he had made."[8] Although God rested from the work of creation, it is obvious that he did not rest from his work of placing his children on the earth. This period of God's labor may have been more taxing than the creation. If all God had to do to complete the creative periods of life was to let life evolve spontaneously, his labor would have been complete on the third day.

The rest from creative labor was the completion of one of the steps in God's plan for the exaltation of man. When we rest from the labors of earthly existence on Sunday, we simply continue with the labors God has outlined for us on his day.

According to this description of the creation, we would expect that labors involving evolution would be curtailed during man's time on earth. (Spontaneous mutation, causing speciation would still continue.) Our schooling in this aspect of creation may have been completed. Our energies were then focused upon gaining experience on an earth that had been completely prepared for us.

In 1977 Singer and Gilbert developed techniques for large scale DNA sequencing and cloning. This made possible experiments such as those already mentioned. Scientists immediately used these techniques to decode genomes from 50 to 100,000 bases in length. The flood of genomes produced by the scientists required such computer centers as GenBank in Los Alamos to be formed to organize the data. A genome consists of chains of adenine, cytosine, guanine, and thymine. These are the nucleic acid building blocks of the genes, the genetic alphabet that spells out different peptides and proteins that make anatomy and control physiology. Another such center, Genex, predicts that the entire genetic code of a human being will be stored in computer disks within our lifetime. (See *Time*, March 20, 1989, p. 62.) By that time it should be more evident to what extent natural selection and intelligent genetic engineering have been involved in evolution.

---

[8] Genesis 2:2.

Complex Behavior

Complex behavior patterns are largely a mystery. The proposal that they are a combination of simple behaviors does not quite do it. John Bonnor of Princeton University suggests that some complex behavior (culture) is a function of the brain and is passed on by imitation, language or signs rather than neurotransmitters, etc., produced genetically. Since complex behavior may be advantageous to the survival of the genes, they have through natural selection produced more complex brains to better compete and cope with environmental changes.[9]

There are, however, some behaviors that do not seem to be simple or cultural. A spider hatched and raised in a test tube can, when released, spin a species-specific web perfectly on its first try. The web building ability is apparently genetically inherited. The spider's nervous system must be programmed to make webs by gene instruction while it is a developing larva. The gene instructions would cause the developing neurons in the brain to interconnect in such a way that a web-building sequence would be triggered by an appropriate stimulus. Could the spider's genes also set up a recognition pattern in the visual cortex so that the spider will immediately recognize a fly as food but a wasp as an enemy? While the web building is likely to be inherited, prenatal development of any animal's ability to recognize enemies, or species specific mating displays visually, seems too complex to be completely genetically controlled.

Each genus of animals has its own peculiar instincts. How does a new-born calf know that it should immediately try to stand up and suckle? A new-born wildebeest calf must stand and follow its mother within an average of seven minutes if it is to survive in an environment of predators. A new-born impala must be able to run within an hour. Such commonplace behavior is taken for granted but it is, in reality, profound. The behavior of the calf looks as if it were carefully rehearsed before birth! But that seems impossible to an evolutionist. How could a calf be trained before it was born? The behavior must be genetically inherited!

An evolutionist will argue that you cannot demonstrate a pre-existence, but then neither can he demonstrate an electron other than

---

[9] *The Evolution of Culture in Animals*, Princeton University Press, 1980.

by the effect it has. The behavior of a migrating bird or new-born calf is also an effect. The choice of cause is genetic or pre-existence. Here again, we try to make the choices mutually exclusive when both are likely correct!

In Genesis 2:4 we find that all plants, animals, and humans were created prior to being placed on Earth. In Moses 3:5 we find that God refers to this as a spiritual creation. We can understand that a great leader on Earth, such as Abraham, was also a great leader in Heaven, but sometimes we forget that animals also had a pre-existence. They were born as spirit animals on the spirit Earth. If we went through a long period of growth as spirits, what do we imagine the animal spirits were doing?

If we can accept the premise that we did the genetic engineering of simple behavior patterns, then we must also have had the opportunity to develop the complex behavior patterns. There may have been several methods proposed, but two seem obvious. One is the development of a multitude of synergistic simple behavior patterns that would be genetically controlled. This method might have been possible, but there seems to be a better way. Spirit animals with well-developed brains could be taught.

Survival Skills

A spirit animal cannot die, so even slow learners were in no danger of starvation as they were taught how to find food or migrate. Birds learned to navigate using polar stars and calves learned to stand up immediately and suckle. This is one reason why the spiritual creation came first. The remarkable behavior of infants was one reason Socrates believed in a pre-existence (see chapter eight).

It should not seem incredible that spirit animals learn and progress. Joseph Smith states, "...all the minds and spirits that God ever sent into the world are susceptible of enlargement" (DHC V, p. 326). If a bird can learn to recognize constellations after birth, could not a spirit bird learn to recognize polar stars before birth? If we love animals here on earth and desire them as pets, would we not delight in training them as spirits? Anyone who has owned a horse or dog can understand that higher animals use their brains for more that instinctive behavior. They can be happy and sad. If complex behavior were entirely controlled by genetics, animals might behave more like robots. One explanation evolutionists have for such behavior is that the whole is greater than the sum of its parts.[10]

Human Instincts

If the concept of pre-existent training is correct, it would be necessary that the memory of pre-existent experiences be more vivid with animals than with us. Perhaps this is one reason why animals do not communicate with us. We have, however, a few nebulous memories that linger with us. Our need to worship a supreme being is often cited as a human instinct, but only because evolutionists have no other explanation for why ancient man worshipped god. To them, the possibility that God or one of his agents actually spoke to man does not exist. We must therefore ask, how does instinctive worship enhance biological survival? The discovery of the importance of the stars as tools of navigation and indicators of seasonal changes very likely occurred before ancient men were awed by their ability to give such directions and think of them as related to a god.

Two often ignored and unexplained phenomena are artistic and ethical man. What connection does the joy of artistic creation have with man's biological survival? Men and women in Russia have risked prison and death for freedom of literary and artistic expression. Men and women have sacrificed their lives for others who were less biologically fit. Why aren't we all like those who disregard others and think only of ourselves? A world that has continually demonstrated man's inhumanity to man ought to be surprised to see so many people try to make life better for others.

Do our genes direct us to insure their survivability? Is a gene capable of sacrificing itself by mutation to increase the probability of the survival of a greater number of other genes? Here the ice gets extremely thin for evolutionary skaters. On the other hand, could it be that our concern for others, and our desire to create, is second nature to us now because it was once our first nature?

Scientists are working to create life and dream of extending life indefinitely. They have tried to communicate with life in other parts of our galaxy. They imagine other worlds with man developed to a

---

[10] For more on this holistic concept of life, see *God and the New Physics*, Simon & Schuster, Chapter Five, 1983, by Paul Davies.

much higher degree of intelligence, having an advanced technology that would make our present efforts seem crude and feeble. Their own probability dictates that an intelligent being capable of creating the solar system and controlling the evolution of life already exists.[11]

Human Sexuality

Human sexuality is expressed both as an instinct and as learned behavior. Sexual attraction and behavior are triggered by the production of hormones and certain anatomical features or behaviors of the opposite sex which may receive different emphasis at different times and in different cultures. Hormonal effects are not pronounced until puberty. This attraction is one aspect of the commandment to multiply and replenish the earth. But male and female role playing begins in the first years of life.

Role playing is very important and is a learned behavior that is needed to channel sexual energy in heterosexual directions.[12] If homosexuality is indulged in, by fantasy or actuality, it can overpower attraction and fidelity to the opposite sex. The concept that a person is born to be a homosexual is false. We are born neutral. It is true that androgens and estrogens are produced at different times and strengths in individuals and may make it easier for some to develop heterosexual attractions. But this is less important than the male and female roles that should be taught and learned.

Male and female role playing is being subverted by TV, magazines, movies, and also by homosexual acceptance. Even though homosexual persons may say that they do not solicit, they cannot avoid being a role model for others. Insecurities may also subvert heterosexual role playing because male-male or female-female relationships may seem

---

[11] The creation of a solar system would be made with existing materials. Such a being would find a place where elements from exploding novas had been compressed—such as on the inner part of galactic spiral arms. Then, a mass disturbance inside the chaotic material would be made to initiate the gravitational collapse of a given volume of the spiral arm. If the gravitational seeds are properly placed in the galactic garden, they will be developed by gravity, in about 30 million years, into a solar system with an earth like ours. A solar system will always be made, but a randomly produced solar system may not have an ideal planet.

[12] Mosaic dress codes were made to help separate the sexual behaviors of boys and girls. Men were required to wear beards which women obviously could not do. Men's hair was not to be as long as women's. It was forbidden to wear clothing of the opposite sex.

to be less traumatic, having provided a measure of security and having met one's needs of acceptance and recognition in the past.

An interesting discussion of this problem must have taken place in the pre-existence. What level of sexual gratification should be established to provide a continuation of each species, including man? (This is another aspect of the commandment to multiply and replenish the earth.) If the gratification level was set too high, it would be hard to resist pre-marital sex and maintain marital fidelity. If set too low, fewer would want to marry and the covenant of marriage would be more easily broken when disputes arose during the first years of marriage.

After some discussion it was probably realized that the level of pleasure and pain should be the same as in other worlds. This might allow the plan of redemption, through the atonement of a Savior, to be more universal. (See chapter eleven.)

Homosexuality

Homosexual sin seems to be harder to overcome than heterosexual sin. The process of repentance is less clear to the offender or to society. After seeing several homosexual men lose their membership in the church, it became evident that their repentance was very difficult. Recently a half-way house, which included sex offenders (Bonneville Center), was established within our ward boundaries. A number of these men were former church members who were anxious to complete their repentance and return to the fold.

This took place during the administration of our former bishop who was informed that one of the men desired to attend church. He arranged for transportation and began fellowshipping several inmates. When I was called to serve as bishop, I began a Home Evening program at the Bonneville Center and asked our High Priests group leader to assign Darrell Hailstone and Clinton Norby to take over the home evening assignment.

I record these names that they might be remembered as two who magnified their callings as home teachers. Through their teaching and fellowshipping, many good men have returned to church activity and some to a restoration of their blessings.[13] They extended their calling to help another ward begin a similar fellowshipping program

---

[13] The process of repentance from sexual sin, such as pedophilia, is long and very difficult. It involves a complete self-realization of all the harm that was perpetrated through many counseling, treatment and analytic sessions. It is a journey through hell, and contains elements of the hell experienced by Alma the younger (Mosiah 27), but the only path to follow to achieve forgiveness. There are such programs, because society recognizes the harm that is being done to innocent children.

I am convinced that homosexuals must go through the same type of program. Unfortunately, society does not yet see consenting adult homosexuality as a serious problem and few effective programs are available. Even if an effective program is free and available, few would voluntarily enter. Some have committed crimes against juveniles which may be exposed and could be punished by imprisonment. While pedophiles do not generally condone or support what other pedophiles do, homosexuals support each other and are accepted by law and media. Their final goal is to get the acceptance of society.

Homosexuals have returned to home and church by loving relatives, bishops and friends. But, without going through exhaustive, humbling, reality-facing self-analysis, they may not be strong enough to refrain from acting out the fantasies that still persist. Fantasies often persist after the program at Bonneville has been completed, but are subdued by a larger vision just as recovered alcoholics have learned to resist the temptation to drink. And, like alcoholics, a few Bonneville graduates will become depressed and revert to their former behavior. And, like alcoholics, some have learned to give pleasing answers that will get them through the program.

I knew an man who had been much admired as an college professor and church leader. He was sought after as a counselor to students and as a church speaker. While many turned to him with their problems, none knew of his homosexual feelings, which he felt no one else could understand or help him overcome. It was only after he began to act out his fantasies that he went to his Stake President. He felt that excommunication might help him face and overcome his problem. After his excommunication, the Stake President, other church leaders and friends extended their fellowship and love for many years, with the expectation that it would not be long before he could overcome his problem and return. His life ended without doing so, to the great sorrow of many. It is nearly impossible for church members to overcome such problems alone without professional help from someone who understands L.D.S. concepts of sin, morality and repentance.

I wrote the following poem to his memory.

> *Higher Ground*
>
> His was a landbound soul
> Sinking near a lifeboat
> Where eager hands reached out.
> But, their clasp seemed more remote
> Than the embrace of the deep.
>
> Time was,
> When others found
> Extended arms,
> When he stood
> On higher ground.

in two other half-way houses and are now working closely with state prison officers.

In our striving to become like God, we need to gain a great deal of knowledge and experience. Somewhere along the way, we must learn how to create life. I am convinced that training began in the pre-existent spirit world and continued through genetically controlled evolution on the earth. Much of what we see as instinct is a product of that experience: genetically controlled simple behavior and survival training of advanced spirit animals.

Chapter Seven

ASSUMPTIONS AND CONCLUSIONS

New Concepts

In the previous chapter on instinct, some concepts were presented on the evolution, or progression, from man to God. Man is seen not as an observer of the works of God, but as a participant, gaining knowledge and experience at every turn. The joy and satisfaction of achievement is ever present. God creates through his children for the sake of his children.

How does one arrive at new concepts? One way is to make an assumption or hypothesis and test it. This is how to "prove all things" as the Apostle Paul counsels.[1] "By their fruits ye shall know them"[2] is the other end of this process, where the hypothesis is seen to be true or false. Before presenting other ideas on the progression from man to God, a few comments on making assumptions and having faith may be in order.

Making an assumption or hypothesis is a useful procedure. It is often the first step one must take to make a discovery. The next step is to see if it remains true under all circumstances. Only then can you say that you have discovered a truth. The problem is that you can never test all circumstances. Thus truth becomes a probability—a statistical assessment. Finding an assumption to be false is much easier, since you only have to find one contradictory fact.

---

[1] 1 Thess. 5:21

[2] Matthew 7:20.

Dark Age Reasoning

During the Dark Ages, nearly everyone assumed that the planets revolved around the Earth in perfectly circular orbits. Their reasoning went something like this:

Assumption: Everything in Heaven is perfect since God lives there.

Assumption: A circle is the most perfect orbit.

Observation: Planets are found in the Heavens.

Conclusion: Planets have circular orbits.

Continuing along the same vein, the following logic showed that the Earth was the center of the Universe.

Observation: Christ was born on the Earth.

Conclusion: The Earth is the most important planet and therefore must be in the center of the Universe.

Assumptions that Simplify

Very little progress was made in astronomy until Copernicus tried to simplify the Solar System by putting the sun at its center. He spent years trying to verify this hypothesis. Later, Galileo saw moons orbiting Jupiter. This was evidence that Copernicus was correct. Everything did not orbit the earth. Some authorities refused to look and others refused to see Jupiter's moons. Later, students and customers using Galileo's telescopes, saw rings around Saturn while Galileo himself refused to see them, because there was no place in his system for such nonsense.

Kepler was an astronomer hired by Tycho Brahe. He studied the position of the planets which Tycho had carefully recorded over many years. Kepler could not make Tycho Brahe's data fit into circular orbits, so he assumed that the orbits were elliptical. Then everything fell into place.

Newton assumed that the earth's gravity ought to extend to the moon and that the moon ought to fall towards the earth just like an apple (except more slowly, since it was farther away) and discovered a Law of Gravity. It was assumed to be 'The' Law of Gravity until Einstein stated a Law of Gravity in more precise terms in his General Theory of Relativity.

Einstein assumed that the velocity of light was the same to all observers, while those moving with a different velocity would be in a relatively different time flow. The result was his Special Theory of Relativity. From the age of sixteen Einstein pondered the nature of light, asking such questions as, "What it would be would be like to travel along a beam of light?" Insight seems to be predicated on pondering.

We are usually on the right track if our assumptions simplify and unify concepts. Most Unified Field equations, relating forces in nature, are not well received because they are too complicated. Complex nuclear structures are, however, necessary in order to give us creations with rich and subtle varieties. Of the four known forces in nature, only complex structures and equations can remotely connect gravity to the other forces, such as in the super-string theories. Contrast this with Einstein's well-accepted and proven equation $E=mc^2$, that unifies and simplifies the relationship between matter and energy.

Assumptions that Mistify

If a proposal can be defended only by stating that it is a mystery, it is probably false. The Triune Trinity is such a concept. It was developed by a committee in Nicaea in 325 A.D. The triune concept of the Trinity is designated a mystery that finite man cannot understand. The question this statement suggests is, how did the finite minds of the committee members (who excommunicated those who disagreed with them) conceive of this infinite mystery when their revelation had ceased with the apostles?[3]

Some broadcast theologians call a religion a cult if it does not accept the Triune Trinity, and many make incorrect assumptions about being saved by grace. Selective scripture testing is done only where evidence is found to support these assumptions.

---

[3] A more modern (5th and 6th Century) commonly used creed in Catholic, Lutheran, and English churches is sometimes called the Athanasian Creed. Athanasius, Bishop of Alexandria, considered to have played a part in the formation of the Athanasian Creed, wrote of the struggle to formulate a concept of deity: "His toilsome and unavailing efforts recoiled on themselves; that the more he thought, the less he comprehended; and the more he wrote, the less capable was he of expressing his thoughts!" (Edward Gibbon, *Decline and Fall of the Roman Empire*, ASM Press, Inc. NY, NY, Vol. II, p. 360.)

Testing Assumptions

Assumptions should be objectively tested as completely as practical. Note the error in thinking that continued through the Dark Ages when it was assumed that the Earth was in the center of the Universe. To people then, it was logical and it obviously supported God. It needed no testing. This may seem an unimportant issue, but Bruno and others did not see it that way when they were burned at the stake for the heresy of not believing it. The following statement illustrates Bruno's inspired conceptions of God and his creations.

> I consider the universe the infinite creation of an infinite divine omnipotence because I think it unworthy of divine goodness and omnipotence to have created a finite world when it would be possible for another, or countless other worlds, to be created alongside this one. For this reason I have declared that there are countless worlds similar to this earth which I, with Pythagoras, regard as a heavenly body similar to the moon and the other planets and countless other stars. I regard all these heavenly bodies as worlds, and their number is limitless.[4]

Giordano Bruno became a member of the Dominican Order in Italy about 1563. By age 18 he questioned the doctrine of the Trinity. When the Inquisition became interested in him several years later, he left the order to avoid interrogation. He was tortured and burned at the stake in 1600 A.D.

False Assumptions

In the Inquisition, we also see a good example of a policy based on a false assumption. The assumption was that control comes by eliminating the opposition, a widespread practice in many countries today. But after 600 years of living in fear and watching relatives and friends die horrible deaths, the people turned away from church authority and in the end the churches of Europe had less support and respect.

---

[4] Walter Nigg, *The Heretics*, p.349, Alfred Knopf Publisher, 1962. Bruno also taught that the Cosmic view was the same from all planets. (Of course, the constellations would be different from each earth.)

The Inquisition also assumed it was its duty to eliminate Satan from the midst of the people in the form of witchcraft. But, as Walter Nigg says, "It is true, the devil was actually involved in this witchcraft affair, he was present in the heart of it, as a cosmic monstrosity. His servants were on the scene, but they were not the legion of the poor terrorized, tortured, and cremated witches. No—what an incredible case of mistaken identities!—his servants had entered into the Inquisitors and judges."[5]

It is hard, if not impossible, to make unbiased observations. We are therefore prone to make invalid assumptions. If we keep our eye on the same fighter in a close boxing match, we will probably pick a different winner than a friend who has been keeping his eye on the other boxer. Just as one should begin with the basic principles of the gospel in order to understand God, so one should order his mind with mathematics and the laws of physics before trying to unravel the mysteries of the Universe.

Archaeologists have discovered stories of Eden and the great flood in Sumerian cuneiform tablets dating back to 2500 B.C. They also know no biblical writings before Moses, ie. prior to 1400 B.C. Therefore, they conclude that "revealing light has been shed on the background and origin of the Bible itself."[6]

This conclusion would hold true if ancient civilizations were in a universal sequence. But, of course, they are not—they are more often parallel than sequential, with a common source. If a younger brother, living in Ethiopia, is found doing something similar to an older brother living in Egypt, can one conclude that the younger brother was taught by his older brother?

If society G is doing something that society E was doing earlier, must it be assumed that society G got its idea from society E? Is there no need to look for societies A, B, or C which may have been a common source to both societies?

Evolution is also the easy way out. Cuneiform tablets reveal that the Sumerians believed in a personal god. Since there was no reference to where that concept originated, the researchers conclude that the

---

[5] *Ibid.* p. 289.

[6] Samuel Kramer, *History Begins at Sumer*, Doubleday, 1959, p. 143.

Sumerians "evolved the notion of a personal God...a divine father who had begot them?"[7]

Have you ever noticed how invariably evolution is used to explain unknown origins? It saves doing research. But the researcher protests, "Why go through all that work and expense when everyone knows it must have happened that way." Does this Dark Age reasoning sound familiar?

We are all aware of how rapidly scientific knowledge is increasing and exposing false assumptions. Less than 100 years ago, many people assumed that intelligent life existed on Mars and the moon. Do you remember when it was assumed that a little fallout from H-bomb testing was not harmful and the destruction of the thymus gland by x-ray radiation was even beneficial? The same knowledge explosion has taken place in archaeology since World War II. *The Sumerian Problem* is a book that devotes 42 pages to changes in concepts, based on incorrect assumptions of Sumerian origin during this century.[8]

We can see that assumptions can get one in trouble unless they are carefully and objectively tested. Are you satisfied, glad, or sad that there are no other procedural options available on the road to discovery? Even when someone tells us something, we immediately make assumptions about the validity of what was said based on comparison to related subjects of experience.

A Perplexing Problem

Let us now examine a perplexing problem by making some assumptions.

Assumption 1: Spirit children were born to our Father and Mother in heaven in a manner and time frame similar to here on earth.

Assumption 2: A spirit child needs tender loving care, just like a child on earth.

Assumption 3: It takes about 150 billion spirit children to populate the earth, including 50 billion cast out of heaven. (Up to the present time there have been about 70 billion people who have lived on the earth.)

---

[7] *History Begins at Sumer*, p. 107.

[8] Tom B. Jones, *The Sumerian Problem*, John Wiley & Sons, Inc., 1969, Part Two.

Before going on, do you see anything wrong with the assumptions?

Conclusion: If God had one wife, it would take 150 billion years to have enough children to populate an earth. If God wanted to create his spirit children, in what is considered the present age of the Universe, he would need at least ten wives.

Can you come to any other conclusion? If the assumptions are correct, polygamy is not a matter of choice in the Celestial Kingdom, it is a necessity. Suppose one God was monogamous and a second God had ten wives. The second God would be able to place his spirit children on an earth ten times sooner than the first God. How loving and considerate would you say the first God was, considering that he made his spirit children wait 135 billion years longer than the second God's children, to receive exaltation?

Let us now add one more assumption and see what happens to the conclusion.

Assumption: There is more than one father of our spirits. That is, although we acknowledge one supreme Father in heaven, we may not all have the same heavenly fathers of our spirits.[9]

Conclusion: Polygamy in heaven may be optional unless it is better to create all the spirit children in a short time.

These assumptions and conclusion are not to be considered as doctrine. They are examples to show how easy it is to overlook alternate assumptions. Another premise is: time flow in heaven is different than on earth. If spirit atoms can move faster than the speed of light, then spiritual time, to accomplish corresponding particle transpositions, would be correspondingly shorter. For example, if spirit particles can

---

[9] Who were all the other Gods mentioned in the Heavenly Council (D & C 121:32), and why is our name for God, Elohim, in plural form? These other gods mentioned are in council about what should be reserved for man at the end of the world. If the gods mentioned were not related to us, why are they involved? In D & C 121:28, we read: "A time will come in the which nothing shall be withheld, whether there be one God or many gods, they shall be manifest." If Adam was one of the Gods in the Council, then some of us could be his spirit children. In the King Follett discourse, Joseph Smith refers to this as a Grand Council, indicating a large body. Brigham Young may not have been too far off track in calling Adam, God. If Adam and the other God's were resurrected celestial beings, would they not have reached godhood? Would they not have Eternal Life, with the ability to have spirit children? What became of those spirit children? Perhaps he did not pursue this concept, due to opposition from Orson Pratt and others. On the other hand, when the Savior prayed he said, "Our father which art in Heaven."

travel 1000 times more rapidly than earthly particles, spirit time would also be 1000 times more accelerated and one could do things 1000 times faster as a spirit.

Moses saw the creation of the earth and all its inhabitants when caught up in the spirit. It seems that some sort of accelerated action would be necessary to accomplish this even if he had forty days in which to do it. In this scenario, the need for polygamy to create the required number of spiritual children would be reduced. The assumption that there are more righteous women than men, if true, would logically require some polygamy to exist.

Making assumptions and testing them is an established method of learning. It is a method that takes time and effort. We are not willing to expend time and effort unless we have some degree of faith that the assumption may prove correct.

Reasoning of Prophets

Some require a prophet to spend his entire life receiving revelations without need to reason. This is a romantic idea that does not come from the prophets themselves. Here are a few statements made by Joseph Smith:

> I *learned* a testimony concerning Abraham, and he reasoned concerning the God of heaven. "In order to do that," he said, "*suppose* we have two facts: that *supposes* another fact *may* exist—two men on the earth, one wiser than the other, would *logically* show that another who is wiser than the wisest may exist. Intelligences exist one above another, so that there is no end to them."
>
> If Abraham *reasoned* thus—If Jesus Christ was the Son of God, and John *discovered* that God the Father of Jesus Christ had a Father, you may *suppose* that he had a Father also.
>
> I want you to pay particular attention to what I am saying...I know it is good *reasoning*....[10]

Let us return to Chapter One and list some statements made by Joseph Smith in the 1830's long before astronomers learned anything about cosmology or relativity.

---

[10] Alma P. Burton, *Discourses of the Prophet Joseph Smith*, Deseret Book, 1956, p. 21.

1. All is one day with God and time is only measured unto man.
2. The earth has been organized out of other globes.
3. This matter was in a chaotic or unorganized state.
4. And as one earth shall pass away, and the heavens thereof, even so shall another come.
5. The pure principles of matter cannot be created or destroyed.

What is your conclusion about Joseph Smith? What is your conclusion about modern science?[11]

---

[11] If the findings of scientists are in harmony with the revelations of Joseph Smith, creationists may have to conclude that scientists discover truths. This indicates that knowledge requires effort—even the study of science—and that D & C 88:79 are not just idle words.

Chapter Eight
FAITH AND KNOWLEDGE

Faith and Knowledge

In seeking truth, God does not expect scientists to discard scientific methods. The Apostle Paul advises, "Prove all things." (1 Thess. 3:21) Alma says, "Behold, if ye will awake and arouse your facilities, even to experiment upon my words, and exercise a particle of faith...your understanding doth begin to be enlightened and your mind doth begin to expand." (Alma 32: 27-34)

It takes time and effort to exercise faith. We are reluctant to put forth time and effort in a project unless we are reasonably sure it will pay off. It takes faith to learn. Without faith, the student will not put forth the necessary effort to master new concepts. A teacher must often lead his students through a mire of basics before the student is capable of creation. If the student does not have faith that the end will justify the means, he will never master the subject. The student may need to see the end product, just as the Savior teaches in the Beatitudes the rewards that follow good works. Students will forget much of what they are taught if they do not have faith that the teachings are important.

It is often difficult to show the end product. How does a teacher know where a student will be in ten years? It is therefore necessary to have faith in a teacher or the system—faith to persist through difficulties. After his resurrection, when the Savior appeared to Thomas, he said, "Because thou hast seen me, thou hast believed: blessed are they that have not seen, and yet have believed." (John 20:29) If we always wait until we are certain, very little will be accomplished. The guarantees Satan wanted in heaven would not only have taken away free agency but also would have lessened the effectiveness of faith. One of our greatest joys comes when faith followed by works comes to fruition.

Is it unreasonable that faith in God should be the first step in gaining a testimony or knowledge of God? The next step is to "awaken our facilities" and "experiment" on God's word. These steps require effort. The fact that many people, including scientists, believe in God, should be sufficient evidence to enable the most skeptical to exercise faith and experiment to see if God exists. Einstein and Newton believed in God. One would think that if the two greatest scientific minds in history believed in a supreme being, evolutionists would be cautious about atheism. The following statement shows how Newton felt:

> The most beautiful System of the Sun, Planets, and Comets could only proceed from the counsel and dominion of an intelligent and powerful Being.

To find out if God exists ought to be enough motivation to cause considerable research. This research is not outside one's field of interest. Whether or not God exists involves each one of us personally. Scientists and philosophers are especially without excuse for not taking the first steps to find out. Why? Because they most likely ponder the evidence of intelligent creation.

The Testimony of Socrates

Socrates had a disciple named Charephon, who was impressed enough with Socrates' wisdom that, during a visit to the Oracle at Delphi, he asked her if Socrates was the wisest man in the world. To his delight, he was told that Socrates indeed was the wisest man. He later related this to Socrates, who responded that there must be some mistake. There were surely wiser men than he in Athens alone.

The search for a wiser man was undertaken by Socrates and a number of his young proteges. As one might expect, his disciples enjoyed finding flaws in the logic of the politicians, philosophers, poets, and artisans. This continued until public humiliation caused the poets, craftsmen, and philosophers to unite and swear out a complaint against Socrates for corrupting the youth, and teaching them of gods not approved by the State.[1]

---

[1] Socrates' defense against the accusation of corrupting the youth was simply that no youth or their parents had been called to testify against him and there were many in the courtroom such as the father of Plato who, if the charge were true, could be called as witnesses against him. His defense against teaching of "Gods not approved by the state" was based on the illogic of his accusers who also accused him of being an atheist.

Even though Socrates presented a flawless defense, he was sentenced to death by a court that had previously made up its mind to find him guilty. During his incarceration he was allowed visitors who urged him to let them bribe the guards so that he could escape to another city. This was possible, because all the Athenians really wanted was to get this gadfly out of their hair. But Socrates said no! He would not leave his home or family or friends. He would rather stay in Athens and die.

Then he told them why. Socrates confided to his friends that he had discovered something truly wonderful he wanted to share with them. He had logically discovered that there was a spiritual pre-existence and now had received an inner witness that there was a spiritual life after death.[2] This had been confirmed by an 'oracle' within him which was a witness to truth. He added that death was nothing to fear and he was looking forward to meeting many, such as Homer and Palamedes, who had preceded him in death.

This account was written by Plato who was present at his trial. Read *The Apology of Socrates,* Plato's account of the trial of Socrates, and *Phaedo,* one of Plato's dialogues, for more detail of Socrates' logic for a preexistence and the manner in which he received a witness of life after death during his trial. There is apparently nothing remaining of anything Socrates himself may have written, although Plato reports that he was writing some poetry while in prison.

We are influenced by the company we keep. Even Newton was so intimidated by other scientists that he delayed publishing his *Principia* for twenty years. The *Principia* is regarded as the greatest book in the history of science. In Newton's day, it was more popular to believe in God and so scientists were not hesitant to include a discussion of God in their conversations. Today, in many scientific circles, it is unpopular to believe in God. Scientists are intimidated by this and so mention God only as a superstition. Recall how the authors of the biology texts referred to God in chapter three.

This change to atheism, among laymen as well as scientists, is almost entirely due to one concept: spontaneous evolution. Many evolutionists

---

[2] Socrates logic for a pre-existence was based on the intelligence of infants. He pointed out that it was not logically possible for an infant to grow so quickly in comprehension based entirely on earthly experiences. Plato, his most illustrious student, continued teaching a pre-existence throughout his life.

see evolution and God as being mutually exclusive. Put in computer language, the *or* gate is accepted, without ever testing the *and* gate. It may be an ego trip for an evolutionist to have no need for God if that makes him number one in the intelligence department and frees him from accountability to anyone except himself.

Research to find God

Suppose a scientist was hired by the governor to do some research on the possibility of an earthquake along the Wasatch Fault. The scientist later reports that there is a 40% chance of a severe earthquake in the next twenty years. When the governor asks the scientist how much time he spent arriving at that conclusion, the reply is "One hour." Do you suppose the governor would question the validity of the finding?

This is where many scientists and laymen would find themselves if asked how much personal research they had engaged in to discover the existence of God. The research is not hard, but it is a challenge and it takes faith to do it right, just as in any other endeavor. Latterday Saints testify that one avenue of research is to read the Book of Mormon. Faith requires that it should be read believing that it may be true. One's faith can be strengthened as he reads this book and asks himself if it would be possible to make it all up. It is my conclusion, along with thousands of others, that it would be utterly impossible to do so. The scope, internal and external consistencies, and profound insights are beyond man's capabilities. Notice, for example, in chapter eleven, how well Book of Mormon scriptures explain the atonement.

The right approach to find out if the author of the Book of Mormon was a prophet is to put aside all preconceptions, such as it's being preposterous that God would talk to anyone, and examine the author by his fruits as the Bible suggests. The only explanation for the cornucopia Joseph Smith left behind was that he was instructed by a higher power. Anti-mormons therefore try to find fault with the way the Book of Mormon came about, such as that it was written by someone else or that it is a waste of time to read a book claiming to be scripture, written by a farm boy. The author has heard ministers on the radio caution listeners not to waste their time reading the Book of Mormon or praying about it—the canon of scriptures has been closed.

After doing the research, the next step is to ponder and pray. Remember that Einstein began pondering the nature of light when he was sixteen. The process—study, ponder, and pray—has worked for millions of people. But the testimonies of others can be an influence only if one hears them. One purpose of bearing a testimony is to increase the faith of others. Some doubt that they could have much influence on a doctor or a scientist, but a logical mind cannot continue to resist truth. In D & C 1:2 we read,

> For verily the voice of the Lord is unto all men, and there is none to escape: and there is no eye that shall not see, neither ear that shall not hear, neither heart that shall not be penetrated.

The Depth of Hell

Origen, a third century religious philosopher from Alexandria, taught that eventually all souls would be redeemed from hell. He believed that we continue to progress after we return to God from whence we came. For such teachings he was anathematized in 543 A.D.

I cannot conceive that the spirits who follow Satan will not eventually be influenced to see the truth by *our* joys and sadness and *our* accomplishments and failures on earth. Thus, even now in this temporary telestial-like experience, we are teaching them. Some day many may see that Satan was wrong. Why do we assume that the only reason they are here is to tempt us?

The fate of the devil and his angels is mentioned in D & C 76:44-48.

> And the end thereof, neither the place thereof, nor their torment, no man knows;
> Neither was it revealed, neither is, neither will be revealed unto man, except to them who are made partakers thereof;
> Nevertheless, I, the Lord, show it by vision unto many, but straightway shut it up again;
> Wherefore, the end, the width, the height, the depth, and the misery thereof, they understand not, neither any man except those who are ordained unto this condemnation.

While Satan and his angels will be denied a kingdom of glory, it seems reasonable that the width, depth and end of the punishment of those who reject Satan, after their earthly experience, would be less than those who did not. Having rejected Christ, revealed by the Father, makes their redemption impossible. The fact that God placed his rebellious spirit children on this earth, observing his other children who are standing on higher ground, is evidence that he expects they will learn a lesson to some purpose.

In his book *Key To The Science of Theology*, p. 116, Parley P. Pratt states that there are many grades of evil spirits, and in the Bible we read of lying, seducing and unclean spirits. If you were God, how would you handle the possibility that some of the spirits who were cast out with Satan might begin to see the light after their earthly experience?

Satan is the prime example of someone who had knowledge without faith. He thought that his knowledge exceeded God's. He lost the faith that he once had—that God knew best. He had a lust for power and very likely for the sensual gratification that he knew was available on the earth. Then, he was denied the body he longed for to fulfill his desires.

The same is true of unrepentant homosexuals and pedophiles. They may rationalize their lust, with intellectual expositions that no harm is being done, but in the end they will be denied children which are the major source of eternal joy.

Chapter Nine
ETERNAL PROGRESSION

There are a few things that are apparently not yet meant to be known. For example, angels have been assigned to guard the way of the *tree of life*. One interpretation of this biblical pronouncement is that science will never discover a way to prevent aging and man will never discover the power of resurrection. Notice that the angels are to guard the "way" of the tree of life. Man has the potential to prevent aging but may be forestalled in reaching that achievement. Most things, however, are meant to be discovered.

Spirit Matter

The nature of spiritual matter is not understood. At present one can only theorize about the relationship between spiritual and physical matter. Spirit matter is not anti-matter or anything detectable. In *God and the New Physics*, (p.72), Paul Davies denigrates the idea of the existence of spiritual matter and concludes that "Nobody seriously suggests that God, or departed souls, have a brain." The idea here is that since nothing detectable leaves the body after death, any existence must be in some other form of intelligence. Joseph Smith states that spirit matter is more refined than physical matter.

Spirit matter may exist in another dimension. Many scientists feel that other dimensions may exist, beyond space-time, which are apparently invisible but potentially interactive with space-time. In order for our spirit to exist with our personality intact, our spirit must have a brain which experienced the same things our mortal brain experienced and have a one-to-one correspondence of all its neural connections. It is possible that a spirit brain could be constructed differently, but it should be easier to resurrect a physical body if it corresponded to the spirit on a one-to-one basis.

It seems unlikely that one's personality could exist in any other form, such as in a computer or cosmic nirvana. In a recent unification theory, six undetectable dimensions exist which interact with space-time. These dimensions are invisible and may have the properties for spirit-matter interaction. That is, if undetectable spirit matter and physical matter interact, it could be in just such dimensions.[1]

Physicists, the ultimate reductionists, explain everything past the first microsecond of the big-bang in terms of known fundamental particles. But neither life nor the big-bang origin can be explained that way, so a holistic approach is used—the whole is greater than the sum of its parts. The physics of the first cause is now a course in philosophy.

The Power of God

Things that are done by God are due to his infinite knowledge and the support he receives from his spiritual and embodied creations. His supreme power comes from these two principles. There are also those in the heavens who seek unrighteous dominion over others.

> All his acts are for the benefit of inferior intelligences. God saw that those intelligences had not power to defend themselves against those that had a tabernacle. Therefore he called them together in councel and agreed to form them tabernacles.[2]

Why is it that God gets nearly universal support and affiliation from the spirits in the heavens? The reason is that God has the program that will benefit them the most. This is somewhat expressed by a verse the author wrote when he was a young man in the U. S. Navy.

The Spirit of God

I feel thy touch upon my soul,
My thoughts rise from the dust,
You guide my steps toward the goal
Where joy is full and all is just.

---

[1] *Superstrings, Scientific American,* Sept. 1986, p. 48.

[2] A. F. Ehat & L. W. Cook, *Words of Joseph Smith,* Religious Studies Cen., BYU, p. 68.

In the beginning was the Word, and the Word was with God, and the Word was God (John 1:1). The Word, of course, is Jesus Christ. Christ is referred to by many names, but is called the Word in reference to "his creative enterprises."[3] The Earth was first spiritually created and is a living soul. The spirit of the Earth is an intelligent creature with power and agency. It obeys God or his authorized representatives. When Enoch moved mountains and rivers, it was the spirit of the Earth that recognized his authority and obeyed his voice.[4] The Lord revealed the following about the earth:

> And again, verily I say unto you, the earth abideth the law of a celestial kingdom, for it filleth the measure of its creation, and transgresseth not the law—
> Wherefore, it shall be sanctified; yea, notwithstanding it shall die, it shall be quickened again, and shall abide the power by which it is quickened, and the righteous shall inherit it.[5]

Powers of Heaven and Earth can only be controlled through righteousness because we are asking help from righteous beings. Ask yourself this question; "If you were the Holy Ghost, would you bear witness to something that was 99% correct?" (Remember, your office is to bear witness to those seeking spiritual confirmation of the truth.) If you did, would you not be bearing false witness to the part that was 1% incorrect?

Many believe that some kind of power goes forth from the hand of God or his representatives to make things happen. May I suggest that what happens is the word of God goes forth and that word is voluntarily obeyed. ("I am the same which spake, and the world was made," D & C 38:3.) God has established eternal covenants with all his spiritual and embodied creations to insure that he will be obeyed and that his

---

[3] Bruce R. McConkie, *Mormon Doctrine*, p.844.

[4] In the 1970's, Jim Lovelock, a biologist from Cornwall England, proposed what is called the *Gaia Hypothesis*. Lovelock said, "The Earth is alive." The idea is not original with him. The Scottish geologist James Hutton wrote in 1785: "I think the Earth is a superorganism." According to Lovelock, the Earth *is* a superorganism in the sense that it regulates itself much as a body does to maintain a constant temperature. The Earth keeps any number of environmental factors nearly constant, including a steady proportion of a highly reactive gas—oxygen—in the atmosphere. The above information is taken directly from *Smithsonian*, May 1988, p. 30.

[5] D & C 43: 31-32.

kingdom shall be a kingdom of order. In D & C 93:17, Jesus Christ verifies that "He received all power, both in heaven and on earth" and in D & C 84:119, "The Lord has put forth his hand to exert the power of heaven."

Those who will not honor their covenants are no longer included in God's Kingdom. Each one of God's creations has the opportunity to grow in power and agency. This is what God covenanted to give them in exchange for their commitment to obey him and help others. Because we have forgotten the covenants we made in the pre-existence, God seeks to establish covenants with us here so that we can again belong to his kingdom.[6] If we live it, the *New and Everlasting Covenant* will give us greater power and agency than we ever had and will give God our commitment that he can count on us to assist him.

When God tells an angel to go down to the Earth and do something, we sometimes forget that angels also have their agency and, like mortals, some have more power and wisdom than others. When God told the three angels to judge Sodom and the other cities of the Dead Sea plain, he knew that they would be influenced by Abraham due to his concern for Lot and his family. The angels knew what a great man Abraham was and debated whether or not they should tell him of their mission. Therefore the Lord said unto them:

> And ye shall have all things done altogether according to the cry of it, which is come unto me. And if ye do it not, it shall be upon your heads; for I will destroy them, and you shall know that I will do it, for it shall be before your eyes.[7]

Creations on Other Planets

One exciting thing about the Kingdom of God is that those who are there can be innovative and creative. The exact same kinds of animals and plants do not have to be formed on each earth. "There are wonderful resurrected creatures in the Heavens that are unlike anything that ever lived on the earth."[8]

---

[6] And the Father teacheth him of the covenant which he has renewed and confirmed upon you. (D & C 84:48.)

[7] *Inspired Version*, Genesis 18:22.

[8] Words of Joseph Smith, p. 185.

ETERNAL PROGRESSION

In his book, *The Timely and the Timeless*, Hugh Nibley makes numerous references to ancient texts describing millions of created worlds. Each world is "different and more wonderful than the other" (p.76). Also, "Every son begets sons, and these in turn consult in the making of 'other worlds' (*Ibid*. p. 80.).

If animals were simply transplanted from another world, why are we deprived of these wonderful creatures? It may also be that we have creatures that they have not seen. This situation would arise if the animals and plants were genetically engineered by God's children assigned to this earth, or if the spiritual creation was a random spontaneous evolution of spiritual matter. Which would be more interesting and instructive to God's spirit children? The major lessons in the creation of life most likely took place in the spiritual creation, since the physical creation must correspond to it. While the spiritual creation may have taken billions of years, the physical creation, being a copy, may have been more readily executed.

Angelic Assignments

Just as a junior executive is trained before he is put in charge of a department, so God works with us. For instance, we may have already had experience in the creation of the Earth and its creatures, and some who were translated or who have finished their second-estate may have had experience in answering prayers. Prayers are heard not only by God but also by assigned angels. These angels do research and make recommendations. This may be one reason why the Lord admonished, "He that seeketh me early shall find me, and shall not be forsaken" (D & C 88:83). It may be that the Lord wants to give the angels time to make recommendations as well as provide the petitioner time to gain new insights during subsequent prayers. In most cases the Lord will honor their recommendations because they are appropriate. Thus they gain experience to become like God. If this is not the case, when and how will we learn to answer prayers? Although some angels may be resurrected beings, they are still striving to become like God. If we repent of our sins, it is these angels who are among the first to know and rejoice. The veil between the earth and heaven works both ways.

It may be that the angel Raphael has a major assignment in presenting the prayers of the faithful to the Lord. Such an angel is mentioned in

Rev. 8:3, and *may possibly* be identified as Raphael in the apocryphal book *Tobit*. Raphael visited Joseph Smith, along with many others who held priesthood keys. Raphael's keys are not mentioned. If Raphael does hold the keys of the *prayers of the faithful*, it is not hard to imagine why his keys were not mentioned. The author's guess is so the Saints would not think that God did not hear their prayers and some would start praying to Raphael. The chapter on Light and Glory presents a concept showing that Elohim and Christ do hear our prayers.

Priesthood in Heaven

In Heaven, priesthood authorities also make recommendations in filling priesthood vacancies on Earth. Thus they assist God and gain experience. We have President Heber J. Grant's testimony that his father Jedediah Grant and Joseph Smith recommended to the Lord that a revelation be sent down to the president of the church to call him to be an Apostle.[9] He was given this revelation when he asked the Lord why he had been called. The same thing happens when bishops, stake presidents, and other leaders are called. How is it that the Stake Presidency, with very few exceptions, unerringly recommend to the General Authorities the man the Lord has chosen to be a bishop? How is it that the General Authorities call the right man to be the Stake President when in many cases they have never before met the man they select?

If there are individual and priesthood organizations in heaven assigned to hearing prayers and making recommendations, do they treat all prayers equally? Is a mother's prayer treated the same as a priesthood blessing? When a prayer is received from the mother, it would be the hearer's responsibility to research the request made by the mother to see if or how it should be granted, knowing that there are many things the mother may not realize. How that prayer is answered may affect many people, some perhaps adversely. When priesthood holders on earth make a request through prayer, or pronounce a blessing, the priesthood in heaven considers the virtue, authority, experience, and inspiration of the priesthood holders on the earth. When inspired by the Holy Ghost, such blessings are recorded in heaven to be fulfilled

---

[9] Spencer W. Kimball, *Faith Precedes the Miracle*, p. 38.

at the appropriate time and manner. In all cases, the principle of living by faith must be carefully considered.

It is important that those holding the priesthood know the will and mind of the Lord and seek inspiration before pronouncing a blessing. Blessings may be pronounced too quickly. Prayer, preceding a blessing, allows for better understanding and inspiration.

During the author's experience as a bishop, he had the opportunity to read two patriarchal blessings that were given by the same patriarch to two young men who were the same age. The first was unusual in its length. It detailed of some of the dangers that the first young man would have to overcome as well as the promises that would be in store if he was faithful. The second was quite general and brief. Knowing that the family of the first boy fasted and prayed before going to the appointment with the patriarch, he asked the second boy about his experience. The young man replied that on the day of his appointment he was watching TV and barely remembered that he had an appointment in time to keep it. The patriarch mentioned to the first family that he was grateful for the spirit they had brought with them and that he felt strongly inspired while giving the blessing.

Proof Without Certainty

In our quest to learn truths, God gives us opportunities to gain experience. We learn degrees of scientific truth by observation with our senses. We must ask whether or not science ever arrives at an absolute truth. Certainly the science of mathematics, though incomplete, is exact. But when we apply mathematics to real-life situations, one begins to wonder. Einstein points this out in the first chapter of a book on relativity.[10]

> By reason of your past experience, you would certainly regard everyone with disdain who should pronounce even the most out-of-the-way proposition of geometry to be untrue. But perhaps this feeling of proud certainty would leave you immediately if some one were to ask you: "What, then, do you mean by the assertion that these propositions are true?"

---

[10] Albert Einstein, *Relativity*, Crown, 1916.

> The concept 'true' does not tally with the assertions of pure geometry, because by the word 'true' we are eventually in the habit of designating always the correspondence with a 'real' object; geometry, however, is not concerned with the relation of the ideas involved in it to objects of experience, but only with the logical connection of these ideas among themselves.
>
> For the present we shall assume the 'truth' of geometrical propositions, then at a later stage (in the general theory of relativity) we shall see that this 'truth' is limited, and we shall consider the extent of its limitation.

Who then has knowledge of things as they are, have been, or will be?[11] Certainly not those who drink shallow draughts. Can the evolutionist, who has drunk shallowly of spiritual things, make judgment about spiritual truths? Can the creationist, who has drunk shallowly of the geology of the earth, make judgments about the details of the creation? In a discourse on God and man, Joseph Smith quoted the following well-known poem.

> A little learning is a dangerous thing.
> Drink deep, or taste not the Pierian spring,
> There shallow draughts intoxicate the brain,
> And drinking largely, sobers us up again.

If you get the idea that scientific 'truths' are tentative and the refining of concepts is an arduous, never-ending task, you are correct. What chance then do we have to gain a knowledge of spiritual things? In the first place, our spirit mind has no clear pre-existent memories and second, our physical bodies tend to dominate our spirits.

Certainty Without Proof

This is a matter of such importance that God assigned one member of the Godhead to spend his entire time revealing spiritual truths to those who seek them. This is private confirmation. Spiritual proof comes to individuals from the Holy Ghost. Thus we arrive at a condition described by anthropologist Ashley Montague:

---

[11] God's definition of truth. D & C 93:24.

> Science has proof without any certainty.
> Creationists have certainty without any proof.

This is somewhat the position of the author. All knowledge I have in science I regard as being extremely useful, but only approximately correct. Some knowledge, regarding the nature of God, I also regard as being approximately correct and, just like science, capable of refinement. I have presented some of these ideas in this book. I know for certain that I am attracted to the earth by gravity. I know for certain that God exists. Yet I know only a limited amount about each. As I learn more about gravity, I find that it is not what I had imagined, being more accurately described as a warp in space-time near an object with mass. Likewise, I gain in knowledge of God, but only by the same kind of effort it takes to learn about relativity.

Truth, the knowledge of things as they are, will remain for a long time an unreachable star. Since all things are interrelated, one can only know truth when he or she knows everything, and it is circumscribed into one great whole. What we strive for are higher degrees of truth. This striving may still continue after we attain Godhood. Why was there a council of the gods when this earth was planned? If God knows everything, what is left to counsel? Who can counsel God? The answer may be that the lesser gods were still learning, receiving assignments, and agreeing to conditions. And as children of the gods, were we present at that council?

Two of the most well-known scriptures in the Church are James 1:5 and Moroni 10:4. These scriptures apply not only to investigators, but to each member. If we do not ponder and pray with the expectation that the Holy Ghost will confirm truths, we either do not believe in him or are not interested in learning the truth of all things. It is possible to learn the truth of all that is lawful to know. Joseph Smith states:

> There are but a very few beings in the world who understand rightly the character of God. The great majority of mankind do not comprehend anything, either that which is past, or that which is to come, as it respects their relationship to God. They do not know, neither do they understand the nature of that relationship; and consequently they know but little above the brute beast, or more than to eat, drink and sleep. This is all man knows about

God or his existence, unless it is given by the inspiration of the Almighty.[12]

As we approach the Millennium, more and more will be revealed to those *seeking truths*.

In Joel 2:28 we read; "And it shall come to pass afterward, that I will pour out my spirit upon all flesh; and your sons and your daughters shall prophesy, and old men shall dream dreams, your young men shall see visions:"

But those who, doing no research, are satisfied just to wait for the Millennium or for the Holy Ghost to reveal all truth to them, may be found ever waiting—but not really wanting.

---

[12] Alma P. Burton, *Discourses of the Prophet Joseph Smith*, Deseret Book, 1956, p. 8.

Chapter Ten

RELATIVITY AND RESURRECTION

Governed by Light

Newton's laws of motion are used to calculate velocity, acceleration, momentum etc. They are simple and work very well as long as you don't go too fast. When objects move very rapidly, one must use relativistic mass to make the laws give correct results. The formula for relativistic mass is:

$$Mr = \sqrt{\dfrac{Mo}{1 - \dfrac{V^2}{C^2}}}$$

Mo = mass at rest
Mr = relativistic mass
V = object's velocity
C = speed of light

This formula has been tested with atomic particles travelling at velocities approaching the speed of light. The results of these experiments verify that the formula is correct and that an object cannot reach the speed of light, since its mass would become infinitely large.

Just as Newton's laws were found to have limitations, it is also apparent that Einstein's relativity has its limitations. Although relativity is used to predict the existence of black holes, it is seen not to be able to completely describe events within a black hole. Einstein's special relativity and general field equations were developed to operate in our world of time and space and have been shown to work accurately within their self imposed limits, which exclude nuclear forces and singularities such as black holes. Einstein made some remarkable relativistic predictions that were experimentally verified years later when scientific instruments were sophisticated enough to make the necessary measurements. This is what brought serious attention to relativity. But we need to realize that Einsteinian relativity does have limits. Therefore, the following arguments are subject to the same limits.

Celestial Speed Limits

In D & C 88:12-13, we find that all things are governed by light. If this light is the light with which we are all familiar, then objects could not exceed the speed of light. Why? Because things that travel faster than light could not be governed by light. Therefore let us make an assumption. Let us suppose that relativity is a universal principle. Suppose that it really is impossible to make an object exceed the speed of light. A most interesting consequence is that God, as a resurrected person, would be limited to sub-light travel from one world to another. This would mean that it would take 100,000 years just to travel across the Milky Way. Could God still be in control of the Universe if such were the case? If one assumes that God is only a local God, the same problems remain. It would still take four years to travel to the nearest star, to say nothing of Kolob which must be more centrally located. But God makes no such limiting statement. He has told us that He and Christ created worlds without number. Joseph Smith states; "There are Gods many and Lords many, but to us there is but one living and true God, and the heaven of heavens could not contain him; for he took the liberty to go into other heavens." (D.H.C. VI, 366)

This information tells us that God must not be limited to sub-light travel. If our assumption about relativistic mass is correct, then we must conclude that God does not possess a material body when he travels from one world to another. So how does he do it? He travels as a spirit. When God created the earth, he did so as a spirit. "And my Spirit moved upon the face of the water; for I am God".[1] It is possible that since Jesus Christ created the earth, he is the one referred to. At that time he only existed as a spirit. But why did God say "my spirit", and add, "for I am God?" If you are only a spirit, and went somewhere, you would not say "my spirit went" but rather "I went." It is possible that God gives us clues to the first creation in the generalities of this creation.

---

[1] Gen 1:2.

Spirit matter is not restricted to obey laws of physics like physical matter. That is, spirit matter obeys the laws that pertain to it, perhaps even in other dimensions. Spirit physics is different from earthly physics. It has to be different, otherwise we would be able to detect spirit matter with our senses and scientific instruments.[2] Spirit matter, therefore, is not restricted by relativity to sub-light travel.

Spirit matter may, however, have some limit in travel and communication. The parable of the man with a field may be an indication of these limits which are summed up in the statement; "Call upon me while I am near."[3]

The Power of Resurrection

Christ had the ability to separate his earthly and spiritual bodies. He also had the power to reunite them. Did he ever have these powers taken away? Did he lose these powers when he resurrected himself? Did he take these powers away from himself? Notice that the following quotation of Joseph Smith refers to the Celestial resurrection of the dead as something to be attained after considerable effort and achievement, not like the passive resurrections of lower kingdoms.

> And you have got to learn how to be gods yourselves, and to be kings and priests to God, the same as all gods have done before you, namely, by going from one small degree to another, and from a small capacity to a great one; from grace to grace, from exaltation to exaltation, until you attain to the resurrection of the dead, and are able to dwell in everlasting burnings, and to sit in glory, as do those who sit enthroned in everlasting power.[4]
> (Ital. added.)

Notice also, the present tense of the following quotation.

> As the Father hath power in himself, so hath the Son power in himself, to lay down his life and take it again...[5]

---

[2] There has to be a connection between spirit and material matter. It's just that we are not permitted to find it. It may be that a Urim and Thummim provides some sort of a linkage.

[3] D.& C. 88:62

[4] Alma P. Burton, *Discourses of the Prophet Joseph Smith*, Deseret Book, 1956, p.8.
[5] *Ibid.* p.11.

Anyone who had that same power would be able to travel through space as a spirit and then clothe his body with the "dust" of the planet he visited—if he found it advantageous to do so. One could pass through a physical wall as a spirit and then reassemble a physical body on the other side. It may have been this process that frightened the apostles when Christ appeared to them after his resurrection. Although the other apostles may have been frightened by the glory of the risen Lord, why would Peter, James and John be terrified of a friendly appearing spirit when they had experience in casting out evil spirits and had seen spirits in glory on the Mount of Transfiguration? Something they were unfamiliar with must have taken place.

In Romans 6:9 we read "Christ, being raised from the dead, dieth no more; death hath no more dominion over him." Some interpret this to mean that Christ's body and spirit will never again be separated. Paul was making a poetic generalization. A literal interpretation would lead one to believe that someone else accomplished Christ's resurrection and that he was once dominated by death. The opposite is the case. Christ had, and still has, dominion over death and accomplished his own resurrection. (No man taketh it from me, but I lay it down of myself. I have power to lay it down, and I have power to take it up again. John 10;18)

For some reason there is a fixation on having the exact same atoms a body was composed of reserved for the resurrection. Would one want to be stuck with 70 pounds of atoms if he died of starvation? Does anyone believe that eating meat will not increase body mass just because the atoms in it belonged exclusively to the dead animal? It can easily be demonstrated that with each breath of air we take, some of the oxygen atoms we incorporate were once breathed by Christ or Adam.

The Resurrection of Joseph Smith

There is reason to believe that Joseph Smith had a resurrected body as early as 1898 when Peter E. Johnson visited the spirit world. He was told that Joseph Smith's body had been resurrected and that when he could do more with his body than without it, his body would also be resurrected.[6] Since the resurrection of the dead began with Christ,

---

[6] *The Relief Society Magazine*, Vol. II, pp. 451-452.

some who merit the Celestial Kingdom, such as Abraham, Isaac and Jacob, have been resurrected.[7] Therefore, it would be reasonable that one of similar stature, such as Joseph Smith, should also be resurrected.

In 1928 the R.L.D.S. Church disinterred the bodies of Hyrum and Joseph Smith and moved them to a new burial site. Their coffins were partially opened and their remains photographed.[8] This has been a puzzle to some people who believe that the exact same oxygen and carbon atoms, of which we are composed at the time of our death, be reserved for us in the resurrection—as if each oxygen atom was different. The disinterment was witnessed by an L.D.S. mission president, but this evidence did not appear to change many opinions about reserved atoms for ones resurrection.

Joseph Smith may also have believed this at one time. He once stated that when little children die they will exist as children with adult intelligences in celestial worlds *with not one cubit added to their stature.* This misunderstanding may occur when we read in Alma 40:23 that in the resurrection "even a hair of the head will not be lost". This might lead one to believe that after the resurrection, not a hair of ones head would be lost *or gained* and no further changes were possible. Luke said "But there shall not one hair of your head perish" (Luke 20:18). The word *lose* may have more than one meaning as in Luke 9:25, "For whosoever will save his life shall *lose* it: but whosoever will *lose* his life for my sake, the same shall save it." It would seem better to interpret the scripture in Alma to mean; "even a hair of your head will not be *missing.*" (*Lost,* however, is more poetic than missing.)

Was Alma really talking about lost hairs, since dead hairs turn to dust? He must have been talking about the loss of the scattered elements of which the hair was composed. If this is your interpretation, then you are changing the meaning of the scripture to one that you believe to be consistent with scientific knowledge, but missing the point—which is one of restoration not of gathering. The authors interpretation seems more consistent with the economy of operation in God's kingdom.

At one time Brigham Young said that the elements of one's dead body would be gathered from the four corners of the world to accomplish

---

[7] D & C 123:37.

[8] Joseph Fielding Smith, *Doctrines of Salvation I,* 200-201.

one's resurrection.[9] Many, perhaps including Brigham Young, were unaware that Joseph Smith clarified his statement *Eternity is full of thrones, upon which dwell thousands of children, reigning on thrones of glory, with not one cubit added to their stature* (HC 6:316). He said that after the resurrection, righteous mothers would nurture these children until they were fully grown. This was published by President Joseph F. Smith in 1918 in the Improvement Era in order to clear up misunderstandings.[10]

Atoms of Resurrection

Suppose it was necessary that your resurrected body be made of the same atoms with which it was composed at the time of death. Suppose further that you died as a baby, was resurrected and then grew to adult form. Would not your body be primarily composed of alien atoms?

In discussing the resurrection, Joseph Smith said; "No fundamental part of one body ever goes into another body."[11] He did not say; "No part of one body ever goes in another?" A logical explanation is that the fundamental part, the indestructible part, would be spiritual element. Joseph Smith also said; "Where was there ever a son without a father, and where was there ever father, without first being a son?".[12] We can all see how we were made of the dust of this earth as we assimilated the elements contained in food which was grown in the ground. How was Adam made from the dust of the earth if Adam had parents?

Adam and the Dust of the Earth

Adam's parents could not have come here to give birth to Adam because Adam was the first flesh on the earth. (See page 34) Being the first flesh has also been interpreted as being the first mortal. But if mortality also included animals, this interpretation does not make sense since dinosaurs etc. had long since died before the last days of

---

[9] *Journal of Discourses*, 8:28.

[10] Duane Crowther, *Life Everlasting*, pp. 252-3, Bookcraft, 1967.

[11] *Words of Joseph Smith*, p. 182.

[12] *Discourses of the Prophet Joseph Smith*, p.21.

Eden. One conclusion is, Adam was a resurrected man who traveled here as a spirit and his physical body was reassembled from the elements of this earth.[13]

Brigham Young indicated that Adam came from another planet.[14] The Bible says Adam was made from the dust of the earth. Both, in my opinion, are correct! Such apparent contradictions have been the excuse some have used to reject the Bible or the church. God has indicated that those inheriting the Celestial Kingdom will have, not the privilege or blessing to come forth, but the 'power' to come forth in the first resurrection. Joseph Smith talks about having the "power of the resurrection pass upon us".[15] Celestial beings must eventually get the power to resurrect their own bodies.

The resurrection of celestial bodies is not the matter-of-fact event envisioned for lesser bodies. The power of resurrection is necessary

---

[13] B. H. Roberts states that an immortal being cannot die. But what about Christ? Mosiah stated that Christ's life was endless, yet it "ended" for nearly three days. The only sense that Christ's life was endless was in that he could have resurrected his body any time he chose, just as he allowed his body and spirit to be separated as he chose. He received the power to do these things from his Father in Heaven. Does he still have these powers today or did someone take these gifts from him? If not, we must conclude that he could lay down his body, travel as a spirit and then clothe his spirit with element any time he chose to do so.

In the Oath and Covenant of the Priesthood, Christ states that he will give everything that his father has given him to those who magnify the priesthoods they receive. Did Adam qualify for such in the world he lived in, before he was asked to come here and temporarily set aside his immortality to begin the human race?

Was Adam and Eve Celestial or Terrestrial? Translated beings are Terrestrial and are ministering angels to planets. As far as the assignment to be the parents of the human race is concerned they probably could have been either Celestial or Terrestrial. But the importance of Adam, the Ancient of Days, the Archangel, the Co-creator of the earth, the father of the human race, and without question one of the Gods in the Grand Council, seems more consistent with Celestial than Terrestrial beings. Celestial beings are independent and have great power and authority to create; Terrestrial beings are dependent and are ministering angels who have not yet reached perfection.

A Celestial Adam would only have to have to lose his memory to lose the knowledge it takes to sustain his physical body, and then partake of something that would cause a defect to allow his physical body to die. A Terrestrial Adam has his physical body sustained by a celestial being, who would simply discontinue that assignment and allow Adam to die after he partook of the forbidden fruit. We can see that a Terrestrial body would have been a handicap during the creation.

In either case Adam and Eve probably traveled here as spirits, and if Celestial, clothed their spirit with the dust of this earth. If Terrestrial, someone else accomplished this "resurrection".

[14] *Journal of Discourses*, 7:285-6.

[15] *Words of Joseph Smith*, p.208.

in order to live in everlasting burnings and to sit in celestial glory. It may well be that only spirit bodies are able to exist in everlasting burnings and when on missions requiring physical bodies, the power of resurrection is needed.

The Ultimate Set of Wheels

After the final judgement, those who inherit lesser kingdoms will have their bodies resurrected by someone from the Celestial Kingdom. But what does that matter as long as you are resurrected? It matters a great deal. If one cannot separate and reunite his body and spirit, he will be limited to sub-light travel! One will not be able to go where God or Celestial beings go. It's too bad the sports car crowd doesn't realize that the ultimate set of wheels is a celestial body.

What makes assumptions exciting is when they lead to the explanation of other things. This makes the assumption much more credible. Have you ever wondered how spirit children can be born to resurrected people? Why do they have spirit children instead of physical children? The "power of resurrection" may provide an answer. Celestial parents may procreate as spirits! Spirit parents bear spirit children. Joseph Smith said; "That the Earthly is in the image of the Heavenly shows that it is by the multiplication of lives that the eternal worlds are created and occupied, for that which is born of flesh is flesh and that which is born of spirit is spirit."[16]

If someone claimed to be God, and had only an immortal physical body, it would be hard to believe that he was telling the truth. Such a person could not be in control of the universe. God's spiritual nature is declared from the beginning, before man could conceive that to be omnipotent one would have to operate at times in a non-physical body.

Op. Cit., p.270.

Chapter Eleven
THE ATONEMENT

Latter-day Saints believe that God loves his children and is concerned about their progress. We believe that God's work is to bring to pass the immortality and eternal life of man. Our ultimate goal is to become like God. This belief requires us to try to comprehend and emulate God.

It is a useful idea to try to anticipate the Lord's actions when reading scriptures or church history. At one time, before the Church was organized, Joseph Smith and Oliver Cowdery were pursued by a mob until Oliver was completely exhausted. Oliver told Joseph to go on and save himself. Joseph then carried Oliver until he too was exhausted. They were in a swamp, miles from home, with a mob all around watching the roads and trails. They were not only drained of energy, but very discouraged. If you were the Lord, how would you have strengthened them as they prayed for help?[1] (Think of a response before reading further!)

Mysteries

One of the most profound actions taken by the God and Christ was the Atonement. How the Savior accomplished the Atonement is a mystery to most Latter-day Saints as well as everyone else. But if the Atonement is of vital importance to us, and a central part of the Gospel, why should this be a mystery? It ought to be one of our most well known and understood concepts.

---

[1] Was your answer one that would give lasting courage, or was it a temporary shot in the arm? The Lord got to the heart of such matters by giving Joseph and others visions of the future of the Church. Their discouragement turned to rejoicing. The profound manner in which the Lord deals with his prophets is unmistakable evidence that their stories are true.

The reason the Atonement remains a mystery to so many people is not only because everyone likes a good mystery, but because it doesn't take research, contemplation, and prayer to perpetuate the concept that something is a mystery. It takes only a closed mind, one that believes that God is mysterious and incomprehensible. It takes someone who believes that he or she can become like God with minimal effort to understand him. In 1 Nephi 10:19 we read, "For he that diligently seeketh shall find; and the mysteries of God shall be unfolded unto them."

In D & C 6:7 God admonishes us to "Seek not for riches but for wisdom, and behold, the mysteries of God shall be unfolded unto you." Where do we find God designating mysteries as forbidden ground? On the contrary, God condemns the pretended mysteries of false priests[2] and the mysteries of the "Great and Abominable Church."[3] Joseph Smith states: "...I never hear of a man being damned for believing too much; but they are damned for unbelief" (DHC VI, 477).

The only problem with mysteries, along with hobbies, sports or entertainment, is that they may monopolize one's time with things that do not pertain to salvation. How many of us are pre-occupied with single activities?

It is interesting to note the language of those who condemn someone who investigates a mystery. A typical statement is that "We should not delve into mysteries," even though everything we do not understand is a mystery. One studies, rather than delves into the lesson, because the condemner knows something about that. How often does the lesson become a reiterated string of historical events in which the pupils spend their time trying to guess the word the teacher has in mind? But that is the safe way to go. None will ever leave the class with a wrong idea to lead them astray. The problem is that few will leave the class with an idea.

Receiving Revelation

God requires even his prophets to research, ponder and pray before receiving revelation. Until the time Wilford Woodruff was President

---

[2] Alma 30:28.

[3] Rev. 17:5.

of the Church, members were being sealed to almost anyone of their choosing in the Temple. Many were sealed to prophets and apostles. Both Brigham Young and John Taylor expressed the feeling that additional revelation was needed concerning the Law of Adoption and Sealing, but it was Wilford Woodruff who received it. This is because it was Wilford Woodruff who was sufficiently concerned to go to the Lord for an answer as he pondered this mystery. He was told that it was proper to honor our parents by being sealed to them.[4]

It is interesting how logical something is once it has been revealed. Apparently Brigham Young and John Taylor were unaware of the words of Joseph Smith in Nauvoo on March 10, 1844; "Seal yourselves unto your fathers."

How does one receive inspiration of the Lord? A righteous life is one pre-requisite. Then does one patiently wait until the Lord sees fit to make something known? President Woodruff's testimony suggests that besides a righteous life, one must study, ponder, and pray.

What was President Kimball doing before he received the revelation on the priesthood? Some condemn President Kimball for pondering and praying over the priesthood problem too long, saying that the stress caused him to imagine that he had received a revelation. His critics wanted a bolt out of the blue. But revelation does not come that way. Nearly all of Joseph Smith's revelations followed prayerful contemplation of an important issue.

Are we like Oliver Cowdery, who thought that all he needed was to ask and it would be given? He was righteous and prayerful, but did not ponder the things he was trying to receive.[5] Perhaps we are among those who are satisfied to wait until the Millennium to gain understanding, but where does God say that he will give us a blessing without effort on our part? Is knowledge a blessing? Are not all blessings predicated upon obedience to law?

Traditions

We pride ourselves in belonging to a church where members are taught correct principles and they then govern themselves. There is

---

[4] *The Holy Temple*, p. 201.

[5] D & C 9:8.

logic in what we do. Why then do we have a fixation on blessing food? Ask someone why he blessed the food before he eats. They will look at you in unbelief and say that they are expressing thankfulness for the food. Then repeat the question. You can give thanks for something without blessing it. If one feels like blessing food, then that may be a proper thing to do. The point is, why single out food as needing a blessing more than other things? Concerning what other item does a family gather several times a day to ask a blessing?

Most families ask God to bless other things besides food. It is living things, especially people, for whom it is most appropriate to ask a blessing. A more significant thing would be for a chosen member of the family to "Offer a prayer" or "Give thanks and ask for needed blessings." Family heads should consider using similar expressions when asking someone to pray, rather than requesting that they "Say a blessing on the food."

It is also common to hear inappropriate phrases in church because someone else has used them. For example, the person conducting may say: "Brother Smith will give us our prayer." Later, when Sister Jones is bearing her testimony, she closes "In the name of thy son" when all along she has been talking to the congregation.

We also repeat phrases to answer questions or to teach. I often wonder what goes on the mind of a six year old child or a 60 year old adult when they are told that "Christ died on the cross so that we may live". Although Christ's death on the cross was the final chapter in his mortal ministry, it was only the final chapter. One can be satisfied to repeat such phrases, or take time to say something more appropriate to the edification of the listener.

We often find ourselves participating in such things because of our traditions. Although we are no less immune to tradition traps than were the ancient Jews, we feel that while ancient traditions were often foolish, ours are sensible. We hold up an artists conception of Jesus Christ in Primary and say, "Who is this a picture of?" I wonder if we would feel a little foolish if Jesus Christ then appeared looking somewhat different? In a bishopric's council meeting with the stake president, a bishop asked if it was permissible to put a picture of Jesus Christ on the chapel wall. The stake president said "yes"! At that time another bishop asked where we could get a picture of Jesus Christ, as he had never seen one. The correct thing to say is that we have symbolic representations of Jesus Christ in picture or even statue form, as in *The Christus*.

People get angry and frustrated when someone questions their traditions, as Christ did to the Jews, because traditions are dealt with on an emotional basis rather than in a logical manner. Our traditions have been stored away, to be used for social occasions, for so many generations that we only vaguely recall their origin and get upset when we are called on to explain our actions. Another member of the council mentioned in the paragraph above was so anxious to defend his traditional behavior that he suggested that the artist which painted the picture of Jesus Christ may have been inspired—as if there were only one picture and one artist.

The Celestial Kingdom

Ask anyone if there is a short cut to the Celestial Kingdom. Before reading further, pause and mentally give your answer!...This is not a trick question; it is a test to see if you have been doing any serious thinking about the Gospel—because there is a short cut. It is the Gospel of Jesus Christ also known as the "strait gate and narrow way"—any other approach will require backtracking. The commandments of God are given to help us achieve success and happiness.

The purpose of the Atonement is well known. The Atonement makes it possible for sinners to be forgiven, on condition of repentance, and therefore to be able to live in God's presence. The condition of repentance is one of the demands of justice. Justice must be satisfied if the Kingdom of God is to remain a house of order, otherwise God's children would cease to honor him as their God. One-third of God's children have previously ceased to do so when they thought they had found a better way.[6]

God's kingdom is one in which true and proven principles are followed. Those who choose not to live by these principles must live elsewhere. This is the bottom line of God's punishment. Hell is the realization that you are living in a world of disorder and frustration instead of the world of order and joy where God is. Hell is a series of abandoned way-stations on the short cut to a utopia that does not

---

[6] D & C 29:36-38; Rev. 12:4-9; Abr. 3:27-28.

exist—a short cut where effort is advertised as minimal and the pleasure principle, maximal.

Do such advertisements exist? Consider the churches that require little thinking, since God is a mystery and the only requirement for salvation is a confession. These same churches free your conscience from guilt. Since all have sinned, if we are guilty of one, we are guilty of all—adultery is no worse than a lie.

Atonement Scriptures

Consider the following scriptures which shed considerable light on the Atonement.

> And thus mercy can satisfy the demands of justice, and encircles them in the arms of safety, while he that exercises no faith unto repentance is exposed to the whole law of the demands of justice; therefore only unto him that has faith unto repentance is brought about the great and eternal plan of redemption. (Alma 34:16)
>
> And now, the plan of mercy could not be brought about except that an atonement should be made: therefore God himself atoneth for the sins of the world, to bring about the plan of mercy, to appease the demands of justice. (Alma 42:15)
>
> I partook and finished my preparations unto the children of men. (D & C 19:19)
>
> The Son of Man hath descended below them all. (D & C 122:8)
>
> It behooveth the great Creator that he suffereth himself to become subject to man in the flesh, and die for all men, that all men might be subject to him. (2 Nephi 9:5)
>
> And he suffereth this that the resurrection might pass upon all men, that all might stand before him at the great and judgement day. (2 Nephi 9:22)
>
> And lo, he shall suffer temptation, and pain of body, hunger, thirst, and fatigue, even unto death, for behold blood cometh from every pore, so great will be his anguish for the wickedness and abominations of his people. (Mosiah 3:7)
>
> He descended below all things, in that he comprehendeth all things. (D & C 88:6)
>
> And He shall take upon him death, that he may loose the bands of death which bind his people: and he will take upon him their

infirmities, that his bowels may be filled with mercy, according to the flesh, that he may know how to succor his people according to their infirmities. (Alma 7:12)

All these things are done that a righteous judgement might come upon the children of men. (Mosiah 3:10)

A Righteous Judgment

These scriptures contain the underlying principles of the atonement. Notice that none are found in the Bible. It is no surprise that the Lord stated that the fullness of the Gospel is found in the *Book of Mormon*, since it is the primary source of this vital message. Salvation and exaltation are centered in the atonement of Jesus Christ.

In order to judge a matter, one needs all the facts. This includes a person's burdens and temptations. Before we can be forgiven, a righteous judgment must be made. Suppose in the final judgment a thief faces the Lord, complaining that he should not be condemned for stealing because his hunger drove him to it, or someone committed suicide because his friends rejected him, or someone sinned because the temptations were too strong, the defense being that one must appreciate and understand the situation before making a judgment. How could the Lord answer if he had not descended below all things and emerged victorious and spotless?

The Lord suffered these things so that he might render a righteous judgment and be able to say to those who had repented and forgiven all others: "I have judged thy repentance and thy sins are forgiven." It is important that we voluntarily subject ourselves to Christ's judgment. We will do this because we will realize that no one else is qualified. Thus "All men might be subject unto Christ." Joseph Smith put it this way, "(in) his inscrutable designs in relation to the human family...we shall all of us eventually have to confess that the Judge of all the earth has done right" (H.C. IV, p. 96). Or as Alma taught:

> We must come forth and stand before him in his glory, and in his power, and in his might, majesty, and dominion, and acknowledge to our everlasting shame that all his judgments are just; that he is just in all his works, and that he is merciful unto the children of men, and that he has all power to save every man

that believeth on his name and bringeth forth fruit meet for repentance.[7]

To confess that Jesus is the Christ is to confess that Jesus is the only righteous judge who can make judgments which are valid in heaven, and that only through him comes forgiveness of sins. No other spiritual leader's life has been shown to be spotless and no such claims have been made, even by their followers.

The logic behind the atonement is sound evidence that Christ is indeed the Redeemer. One can see that if conditions in other worlds are like ours, the atonement might also be applicable to them and the Lord could be the Savior to many worlds.

Parallel Worlds

If ten percent of Eloheim's spirit children became celestial Gods, and if they procreated spirit children at a rate of one every two years, about forty billion billion spirit children would exist after five billion years, the age of the solar system. This would be enough to populate two hundred million worlds.

The supervision of the construction of these solar systems would be by God or his first-born spirit children that had the knowledge and power to do so. Christ stated that he created worlds without number, and certainly no man can number these worlds which are predicted to exist. It would be likely that all of these worlds would exist in the same galaxy, and in the Milky Way Galaxy of one hundred billion stars, only one star in five hundred would be needed to serve as a sun to a world like the Earth.

This answers the problem of why Christ could have created so many worlds but came to only one to receive a body and accomplish the atonement. The worlds were not all in sequence but more nearly parallel in existence. Christ could be the Savior to all within this galaxy.

These parallel worlds are also inhabited by some translated beings who are ministering angels and at the same time possibly becoming strong enough to overcome some of the problems of the flesh that still existed when they finished their mortal life on other planets. Translated beings from other planets may have lived here, or may do so during

---

[7] Alma 12:15

the Millennium. Recall in Genesis 19:1-3, Abraham fed cakes, meat, butter, and milk to his angelic visitors who were on their way to judge Sodom. *And he made them a feast, and did bake unleavened bread, and they did eat.*

Joseph Smith states:

> Many have supposed that the doctrine of translation was a doctrine whereby men were taken immediately into the presence of God, and into an eternal fullness, but this is a mistaken idea. Their place of habitation is that of the terrestrial order, and a place prepared for such characters he held in reserve to be ministering angels unto many planets, and who as yet have not entered into so great a fullness as those who are resurrected from the dead. "Others were tortured, not accepting deliverance, that they might obtain a better resurrection," (see Heb. 11:35).
>
> Now it was evident that there was a better resurrection, or else God would not have revealed it unto Paul. Wherein then, can it be said a better resurrection. This distinction is made between the doctrine of the actual resurrection and translation: translation obtains deliverance from the tortures and sufferings of the body, but their existence will prolong as to the labors and toils of the ministry, before they can enter into so great a rest and glory.
>
> On the other hand, those who were tortured, not accepting deliverance, received an immediate rest from their labors. "And I heard a voice from heaven, saying unto me, Write, Blessed are the dead which die in the Lord, from henceforth:...they may rest from their labors and their works do follow them." (Rev. 14:13) They may rest from their labors for a long time, and yet their work is held in reserve for them, that they are permitted to do the same work, after they receive a resurrection from their bodies. But we shall leave this subject and the subject of the terrestrial bodies for another time, in order to treat upon them more fully.[8]

Paul Davies supposes that Christianity could not accept the idea that life may exist on other planets. He states,

---

[8] Alma P. Burton, *Discourses of the Prophet Joseph Smith,* Deseret Book, 1956, p. 31.

The existence of extra-terrestrial intelligence would have a profound impact on religion, shattering completely the traditional perspective of God's special relationship with man. The difficulties are particularly acute for Christianity, which supposes that Jesus Christ was God incarnate whose mission was to provide salvation for man on earth. The prospect of a host of 'alien Christs' systematically visiting every inhabited planet in the form of the local creatures has a rather absurd aspect. Yet, how otherwise are the aliens to be saved?[9]

The Laws of Heaven

The laws of heaven help us progress socially and intellectually. When we keep them we are rewarded by progress and continuance in our heavenly society. The laws of heaven also include laws governing redemption when the laws are broken. These are the laws of mercy and justice. If we sin, we lose our place, and unless we submit to the laws governing redemption, we will remain cut off from the presence of God.

Justice demands that redemption incorporate the following:

1. Repentance—including forgiving others & restitution.
2. A righteous judgment to see that the conditions of repentance are satisfied.

Justice demands that the righteous judgment could only be the product of an infinite atonement, which includes a complete (infinite) understanding of physical and spiritual temptation and suffering. But the charity of the one chosen by God to become the Savior, and apply this righteous judgment to God's repentant children is also necessary. This is the mercy that can satisfy the demands of justice. Mercy is the action necessary to bring about the redemption of a fallen soul. We read in Alma 42:22, "But there is a law given, and a punishment affixed, and a repentance granted; *which repentance mercy claimeth;* otherwise justice claimeth the creature and executeth the law,..." Mercy is one of the attributes of God's grace. Thus, we are saved by grace.

It is not productive to monopolize one's time on concepts which have little to do with the quest for eternal life. Some waste time finding

---

[9] Paul Davies, *God and the New Physics*, p.71.

fault, or speculate on irrelevant things as what Christ might have been doing as a youth. Apostates are always looking for some new secret to show that they are the enlightened ones.

The problem in doing research is trying not to interpret findings only to support your hypothesis or preconceived notions. This might have been one reason that God called Joseph Smith when he was so young. A more serious problem, however, is doing no research at all.

Chapter Twelve

LIGHT AND GLORY

Forces

One of Einstein's dreams was to relate known forces in nature with simple mathematical expressions. The attempt is still being made. If you were God, describing to man the forces through which you operated, how would you proceed? Would you describe electromagnetic force, the force of gravity, and weak and strong nuclear forces? How would you describe your method of communication throughout the universe without depriving your children of the joy inherent in the discovery of such things?

These forces are seen by scientists to be interrelated. The one we are most familiar with, and the only one the ancients knew about, was light—electromagnetic radiation! It is the force through which we gain information by means of our senses. Using light as a general term for electromagnetic energy, one may say that we see with light, we hear with light, and we feel with light. Sounds exist because electromagnetic fields within atoms are compressed as a molecule collides with its neighbor to pass on sound energy. Our sense of touch exists through electromagnetic impulses in neurons. Our energy is obtained and expended through electromagnetic exchanges in molecular bonds. Not only is our brain activated through electromagnetic impulses from our sense organs, but if our brain is to be activated by spiritual communication, electromagnetic energy must be expended, since this is the energy by which it operates.

Thus, electromagnetic energy appears to be related to the light of God—it's use correlates with the purpose for the light of God. If the unified field concept is correct, then light is related to all other forms of energy. Thus, not only do we become enlightened and quickened with light but the planets and stars are governed by a cousin of light which we call gravity. Joseph Smith stated that "God had materials to organize the world out of chaos-chaotic matter, which is element, and in the which dwells all the glory." Chaotic matter is characterized by the radiation it produces. Thus, radiation and glory are related.

Spiritual Eyes & Ears

Our spirit is in the likeness of our body. We have spiritual eyes and ears. Why then do they not work? Why cannot our spiritual eyes see the spiritual world they once were able to see? One explanation is that our spiritual senses are completely overwhelmed by their confinement within a physical body. Only great faith could overcome this confinement. Another explanation is that we are prevented from using our spiritual senses by commandment. This would be similar to hypnotism except that it would last until our spirit is separated from our body, whereas hypnotism is a temporary condition. When we die we apparently still do not remember our pre-existence. We will still be under some constraint not to do so. Those who have visited heaven and returned did not have their pre-existent memories returned while they existed as a spirit. Those who have not yet merited the Celestial Kingdom, will likely work toward a kingdom of glory until the end of the Millennium. The principles of testimony and faith will still be operative in missionary work in heaven, just as they are on earth. If those who die remembered their pre-existence, there would be no need for missionaries. (See also, the comments on Terrestrial bodies in chapter eleven.) Our pre-existent memories will likely be returned after our resurrection.

If our spirit were completely bound by our physical body, then there would be little purpose for having our spirit within us. But there is constant communication between our physical and spiritual brains. When we die, all the sensory and cognative knowledge contained in our brain is saved because it is also part of our spiritual brain. On the other hand, the transfer of information from spirit to mortal brain takes place on a subliminal basis. Thus we are influenced by our spirit in a subconscious way, allowing us to still operate on principles of faith. This also allows input from other spirits. The degree to which we recognize this varies from zero to a complete sensory manifestation.

But direct manifestations are not given without a very important reason, since they negate the principle of faith by which we should live.

When I was about twelve years old I received a 'verbal' warning from a personage whom I suppose was an angel. I heard a voice but saw no one. I did not hear the voice with my natural ears. The voice was heard within my head. It was a male voice speaking with benevolent authority. His voice was so compelling that I obeyed him immediately. I did not realize that anything extraordinary had happened until I arrived home a few minutes later. The warning was, not to accept the invitation of my 'friends' who were assembling in a secluded place to indulge in a sin for which Sodom was destroyed.

Most of us are able to receive only one bit of information at a time. Pain can be obsured if we overload our brain with other sensory signals, such as noise. In some ways we are like a computer with a serial port. Our eyes can only focus on one small area of vision at one time— about the size of a written word at normal reading distance. This limits the input of visual information. Perhaps this is also why we can think of only one thing at one time. Spirit brains are apparently not limited in this way.

The transfer of one bit of information from a computer to a magnetic tape requires about one billionth of a watt-second of energy. The energy our senses require to transfer the same amount of infomation is about one billion times less. But if we were to listen to the words of all five billion people on the earth, the total energy input would be one-hundred times greater than the threshold of pain.

Now apply the same reasoning to the reception of visual information and multiply this input by the beings in the number of worlds from which God receives information and you can easily see that God would have an input and corresponding output of energy that would be way beyond the tolerance level for a mortal person. One's body would quickly be destroyed in the presence of God.

The Glory of God

Joseph Smith states: "God Almighty himself dwells in eternal fire; flesh and blood cannot go there, for all corruption is devoured by the fire." (H.C. VI, 366) Why does God choose to dwell in eternal fire? God might dwell there to exclude corruption from evil beings who could not tolerate living there. But it is also possible that the eternal fire is due to communication to and from all his creations.

> And the light which shineth, which giveth you light, is through him who enlighteneth your eyes, which is the same light that quickeneth your understandings;
> Which light proceedeth forth from the presence of God to fill the immensity of space—
> The light which is in all things, which giveth life to all things, which is the law by which all things are governed, even the power of God.[1]

This is one explanation for the statement that "The glory of God is intelligence."[2] What scripture leads one to believe that God gloried in his own intelligence even though his intelligence is of prime importance? Bringing to pass the immortality and eternal life of man would add more intelligent communication with God and would thus add to this glory. Only those who were 'one' with you can add to your glory, since only such will wish to communicate with you.

Celestial Communication

In the great intercessory prayer in Gethsemane, Jesus said, "And now, O Father, glorify thou me with thine own self with the glory that I had with thee before the world was." (John 17:5) Then in verse 22 Jesus continues, "And the glory which thou gavest me I have given to them; that they may be one, even as we are one..."

What is the Lord asking for? Is it honor or recognition? If so, how do honor and recognition make the apostles 'one,' as are the Father and the Son? Being 'one' is thought of as being one in mind and purpose. What would make 'oneness' more complete than to establish spiritual communication with God's creations? This cannot be done without the accompanying glory that goes with it and would endow one with honor and recognition. Perhaps one reason why the countenance of Moses continued to shine after the descent from Mount Sinai was that he was still in communication with the celestial kingdom. Notice that even

---

[1] D & C. 88:11-13.

[2] D & C. 93:36.

though the whole body of Moses was in the presence of God, it was only his face that was shining.[3]

A Celestial sphere is a receiver and transmitter of intelligence —a gigantic Urim and Thummim. Note that "Light proceedeth forth from the *presence* of God to fill the immensity of space."[4] Each celestial being will have his own crystal Urim and Thummim to aid in his communication with other spheres.[5]

In the *Doctrine and Covenants* section referred to above we find a connection between glory and the reception of information:

> Angels reside in the presence of God, on a globe like a sea of glass, where all things *for their glory are manefest,* past, present, and future, and are continually before the Lord.
>
> The place where God resides is a great Urim and Thummim.

It almost sounds as if Urim and Thummim mean receiver and transmitter. Each individual Urim and Thummim will be coded with the owner's secret name, perhaps like a computer entry code. It appears that even a celestial brain needs assistance in receiving information from distant sources. Then we shall *see as we are seen* (H.C. VI, 476).

A large Celestial sphere could be tuned to a certain carrier frequency and operate like a gigantic antenna.[6] Small individual Urims and Thummims could modulate or demodulate this carrier wave and tune in to whomever you wanted. Perhaps, as one progressed, he or she could communicate with more and more people at the same time. All things are before God. (D & C, 88:40-45)

The only problem with this theory is that it takes away some of the mystery of the Urim and Thummim and makes God seem dependent

---

[3] In Akkadian Mesopotamian legends, such as the Creation Epic, we find that apparently every god possessed a "melammu" emanating from his head....The word came to denote a crown of glory.

[4] D & C, 88:12.

[5] D & C, 130:7-10.

[6] A large physical sphere, such as a sun, oscillates at a very low frequency. High frequencies are required to transmit large amounts of information. A spirit sphere, near to Kolob, would have to provide a carrier wave with incredible capacity. A planet would have to be massless to operate at such a high frequency, which is precisely the property of spirit matter. Kolob, on the other hand, would have to be very massive in order to control other planets by gravitational force. Notice in Abraham 3:2-9, that the throne of God is not on Kolob, but near it.

on external devices. It may be that God does need a Urim and Thummim to hear our prayers, or else the Urim and Thummim is only needed to assist those who have not reached the status of Godhood.

God instructs angels to descend to the earth and carry out his directives. He then requires them to report their stewardship. This seems to be the meaning of Jacob's vision of the ladder which went into heaven, on which angels were descending and ascending.[7] This does not mean that God only knows what is going on through his angels. Angels are still progressing to become like God, and are gaining experience. The fact that God's glory cannot be tolerated by mortals is evidence that he does, indeed, hear our prayers. The radiation that procedes from God, to communicate with and control his kingdoms, must also return. You can accomplish very little if you do not know the results of your directives.

---

[7] Genesis 28:12.

Chapter Thirteen
IF YOU WERE GOD

The Joy of Discovery

We recognize Frank Lloyd Wright as a builder of unique homes and buildings, but we also know that he probably did not pound a single nail in any of them. We credit God as the builder of the world and man. In this book we see that God may have given his children the opportunity to genetically engineer the creation and evolution of the earth's plants and animals. In the Biblical account of creation of the earth's flora and fauna we see that God typically says, "Let the waters bring forth," or "Let the earth bring forth," but as to man God says, "Let us make."

The communication between God and Adam in the Garden of Eden demonstrates an interesting relationship between God and man. God tells us the essentials, then leaves the rest up to us. He offers us inspiration, and then verification when we are on the right track. Our joy of discovery is never disregarded.

The Language of Adam

We read in Genesis 2:19-20 that it was not God who gave names to the animals that were created, but Adam. It is only reasonable that Adam, having been given a major assignment in creating the animals of this earth, should have also been given the privilege of naming them. Adam likewise was given the problem of finding a way of recording such names. This is a conclusion based on the following paragraphs.

If the earliest records we have from the descendants of Noah are an indication of the invented written language of Adam, it would seem that Adam used a single symbol, or a combination of symbols, for each word. This seems to be pictographic writing at first glance, but was evidently more sophisticated. At first glance Egyptian heiroglyphics seem to be pictographic, but contain elements of grammar and syntax as complex as our own, even giving information on how the words were to be pronounced.

The descendants of Noah were combining written characters to give multiple meanings. This was done by preceding a character with an unpronounced determinative, so you could tell if the character meant plough or ploughman, for example. They also added an unpronounced character at the end of some words, called a phonetic compliment, to give the word ending the correct pronunciation. This practice may have originated with Adam and could easily record genealogies, but would be cumbersome for detailing an account of the creation.

While northern kingdoms stamped out crude cuneiform characters on clay with a stylus, the Egyptians drew beautiful hieroglyphics with red and black ink on parchment and papyrus. The record of such combined ideographic characters is found continuing only for a short time before a major breakthrough in the written language took place. This short record of ideographic character writing is readily explained by the Biblical flood and Noah's descendants, but not by evolution.

Earliest Writing

This earliest known writing comes from about 3,200 B.C. and is called Sumerian. The record of this early ideographic written language in Mesopotamia continued only a short time after the arrival of the Sumerians who were, very likely, primarily descendants of Shem.

Although archaeologists refer to these characters as pictograms, they are not pictograms. Those who have studied these characters cannot read them as pictograms, which should tell the same story to everyone. Evolutionists would like nothing better than to find a history of the development of pictographic writing, but have been unable to do so, although several thousand such pictographic characters have been found in the ancient Sumerian language.[1]

The revolution in writing took place to reduce the number of ideographic characters. This revolution is well documented. The

---

[1] Hugh W. Nibley, *Nibley on the Timely and the Timeless*, Religious Studies Center, BYU, 1978, p. 107.

Sumerians and their descendants, such as the Assyrians, Babylonians and Hebrews, may have been the ones referred to as having one language and one speech in Genesis 11:1. It was about this time that the "earth was divided.[2] This major step in the reformation of the written language came when the "ideographic characters" began to be used as syllables and consonants and it seems to have taken place about the time of the Biblical Tower of Babel.[3]

It is evident that there was no agreement among the scattered kingdoms, such as Ebla, Ugarit, and Akkad, or even within each kingdom, on how this should take place. Each kingdom saw the opportunity to develop their own language. Why? Pride, and perhaps the reason that the Nephites had a special written language for recording sacred history and God's communications to them.[4]

---

[2] Genesis 10:25. In D & C 133:24 we read "And the land of Jerusalem and the land of Zion shall be turned back into their own place, and the earth shall be like as it was in the days before it was divided." Here we see that a divided *earth* is just a divided *land*. Even today, we speak of the subdivision we live in. We also see that the land of Jerusalem shall be like it was before it was divided. Clearly the Mount of Olives is still near Jerusalem and no major geographic changes have taken place since Old Testament times. The implication is that the people were divided into the land or in other words, scattered. It is clear from sound geological evidence, such as the way mountain ranges were formed, that the continents separated from each other 200 million years ago.

In Genesis 10:32, and 10:5 we read, "These are the families of the sons of Noah, after their generations, in their nations: and by these were the nations divided in the earth after the flood." "By these were the isles of the Gentiles divided in their lands; every one after his tongue, after their families, in their nations."

These last two scriptures indicate that the division of the lands was accomplished by people moving to new locations, rather than a movement of the earth's crust."

[3] It is not clear who the genius was who originated the idea of syllabic writing but many believe it was a Sumerian. Most authorities believe that it only happened once.

[4] "And a book of remembrance was kept, in the which was recorded, in the language of Adam, for it was given unto as many as called upon God to write by the spirit of inspiration; And by them their children were taught to read and write, having a language which was pure and undefiled." (Moses 6:5, 6)

Here we are talking of a group of righteous people who were speaking the language of Adam, rather than the language of God. Adam is given credit for the language. It is also evident that others had defiled that language. It seems that some of Noah's descendants used the pure Adamic language and some did not. In *Mormon Doctrine*, Bruce R. McConkie states that the Brother of Jared spoke the original and pure language. (p. 19) The oral languages would likely be similar, except for corrupted words in some locations, until the time of the confusion of tongues.

"Linguistically, the structure of Sumerian stands out today with unusual clarity and transparent inner logic..." (*The Sumerian Problem*, Tom B. Jones, John Wiley, 1969, p. 96.) This is an

At the time Lehi left Jerusalem, hieratic and demotic, cursive forms of Egyptian hieroglyphics, were undoubtedly well known to Lehi and his family.[5] It would have been a simple thing to record their sacred history in demotic. Instead, they "reformed" the Egyptian into a new language that no outsider could understand.[6] While this may have also been done to save space (*And it came to pass*[7] could have been written with a single symbol), it kept sacred things from being profaned and effectively prevented unauthorized persons from altering the document—as was done with the Bible. The bulk of Lehi's descendants apparently did not learn this language and left their record on stone in an entirely different form.

Modern examples of religions using a sacred language for religious purposes are the Copts and Buddhists. The Copts are a a branch of the Eastern Orthodox Church and use Coptic in their religious writings and translations of the Bible. Coptic is the ancient Egyptian language written in Greek. Without Coptic, some of the sounds of the ancient Egyptian language would have been lost forever. The sacred books of the Buddhists are preserved in Pali, the language of their founder, Siddhartha Gautama who lived about 500 B. C.

With selected characters being used as syllables and consonants, the number of characters in Ebla were reduced to about two hundred. The idea of using syllables and consonants was a brilliant stroke of genius comparable to the genius of Newton or Einstein. Vowels followed later. Much of the writing in Egyptian was soon done entirely with consonants similar to our own alphabet. It was only when Champollion realized that the hieroglyphs on the Rosetta Stone were phonetic, rather than pictograms, that he was able to translate the ancient Egyptian language.

---

amazing statement about the most ancient language known. The title of this reference book results from the fact that archaeologists do not know where the Sumerians came from or why their language was so well developed. But they are recognized as being in Mesopotamia first and the inventors of written language. Their own legends say that they came from the sea which gave birth to the earth. (Archaeologists suppose, therefore, that they came from the Persian Gulf, the only access to the sea. In doing so, they ignore other legends such as *Enmerkar and the Lord of Arrata*, which tells of earlier, northern, mountainous relations.)

[5] Mosiah 1:4.

[6] Mormon 9:34-35.

[7] *And it came to pass* is a common expression in Chontal, a Mayan dialect. It is written simply as *ut*. *The Messiah in Ancient America,* Warren and Fergusen, Book of Mormon Research Foundation, 1987, p. 62.

A more detailed account of this revolution in writing can be seen in *A Revelation in Archaeology,* by Chaim Bermant. On page 120 we read:

> There were remarkably many differences between the values which the characters could assume in different areas, and even in the same area at different times. A possible explanation is that when the idea of using the Sumerian characters for Akkadian syllables first developed, different Akkadian-speaking areas worked out their own detailed solutions to the problem of which syllabic values should be assigned to which characters.

As an example of the confusion within the Akkadian culture, the word for mouth "acquired such values as ka, ga, qa, pi, and pe—though at no time and place were all five available."[8] Akkad (Accad) was one of Nimrod's cities.[9]

The Confusion of Tongues

The confusion of tongues was therefore not only due to the written languages developed by each city, but also to the confusion or disagreement among the people within cities. Jared and his family were aware[10] of the confusion that was taking place and asked God to bless them so it would not happen to them.[11] This was accomplished by leading them to a land where "never had man been" (Ether 2:5).

This discovery is another verification of the Biblical account. The confusion and appearance of different languages, perhaps being a little different from what we had imagined from the biblical account of Nimrod's Tower of Babel, is remarkably there.[12]

---

[8] *A Revelation in Archaeology,* Chaim Bermant, Times Books, p. 120.

[9] Genesis 10:10.

[10] Ether 1:34.

[11] See Hugh Nibley, *The World of the Jaredites*, p. 165, for another discussion of the confounding of the languages at the time of Babel. See also, *The Jaredites,* Mark E. Petersen, Deseret Book, p. 9.

[12] The first impression you get when you read the Bible is that Nimrod built his tower to *reach heaven,* although you might wonder why he did not just climb a mountain. It is more likely that he wanted to build the highest tower in the land to honor the god of his city and bring glory to himself. The most powerful god would, of course, live in the highest city temple, *nearest to heaven.* He would be "The Most High God." Many, from other cities, would be

If God named the animals and provided all of Adam's descendants with an efficient system of writing, we would have seen a well developed system of writing from the beginning and would have been astounded that the earliest writing had, say, only two dozen letters. It is worth noting that the biblical record of the creation was not written by Adam, one who was once much involved with it, but by Moses later on when the written language was well developed.

Enoch made a record of the events and genealogies of Dispensation of Adam. Enoch seems to have been the first historian.

In the Doctrine and Covenants we read:

> And Adam stood up in the midst of the congregation; and, notwithstanding he was bowed down with age, being full of the Holy Ghost, predicted whatsoever should befall his posterity unto the latest generation. These things were all written in the book of Enoch, and are to be testified of in due time. (D & C 107: 56-57)

In the Pearl of Great Price we read:

> And a book of remembrance was kept, in the which was recorded, in the language of Adam, for it was given unto as many as called upon God to write by the spirit of inspiration;
>
> And by them their children were taught to read and write, having a language which was pure and undefiled.
>
> Now this same Priesthood, which was in the beginning, shall be in the end of the world also.

---

drawn to Nimrod's tower and god, and it would tend to keep other from leaving (Gen. 11:4). This would increase Nimrod's authority in religious matters and subsequently give him more power to restrict religious freedom as far away as Ebla.

Nimrod was jealous of the Priesthood, which was denied him. He had great popularity and power. All he lacked was complete religious authority. There are several references stating that Nimrod stood on top of his tower and shot an arrow into the heavens killing the rival god (of the Hebrews?).

The tower of Babel was probably a zigguart, which was a staged tower with a temple at the apex, such as those in Central America. This was spoken of as the "Bond between Heaven and Earth." The temple at the top of the tower was called *The House of God* or *The House of the Mountain.* The word "mountain," as used then, had a deep religious significance and we are reminded at once of Isaiah 2:2 where we read that the "Mountain of the Lord's house shall be established in the top of the mountains, and shall be exalted above the hills; and all nations shall flow unto it." It is interesting, and perhaps significant, that the Manti temple site, dedicated by Moroni, was a hill.

Now this prophecy Adam spake, as he was moved upon by the Holy Ghost, and a genealogy was kept of the children of God.

And this was the book of the generations of Adam,.... (Moses 6:5-8)

A language that is pure and undefiled brings to the romantic mind a language that has an elegant phonetic alphabet and is perfect in all of the elements of grammar. The scriptures, however, describe the Adamic language primarily recording genealogies that Adam's descendants could read. A short time later we find Jared writing in a language that no one could read without the Urim and Thummim (Ether 3:22). It is possible that Adam also made such a record.

In *Mormon Doctrine* (p. 818), Bruce R. McConkie suggests that the Urim and Thummim was undoubtedly used before the flood. Urim and Thummim languages and records had no effect on the development of the common language of the people. The Urim and Thummim could be used to write a unreadable record, revealing to the writer a special written language reserved for that purpose, or require the inventors of the written characters to be the one through which the written concepts were revealed to the reader. The latter procedure seemed to be the case with the *Book of Mormon*. Communication between God and man seems to take place in man's language.

> Behold, I am God and have spoken it; these commandments are of me, and were given unto my servants in their weakness, after the manner of their language, that they might come to understanding. (D & C 1:24)

The Urim and Thummim is like a modem through which sacred writers and creators reveal concepts to *seers*. A pure and undefiled language may simply refer to a language which contained no degrading or un-godly elements rather than one with which one could express every nuance of meaning.

The roots of the confounding of the Tower of Babel language took place when God required Adam to name the animals and invent his own system of writing. When the various communities got the idea of syllabic writing, the Sumerian (Adamic?) mother tongue was quickly lost. (There is a good possibility that Sumerian was the language of Shem. See chapter 4.) How does the atheistic student of ancient languages explain the single source of the ancient languages or even the Biblical statement that Adam, not God, named the animals? How remarkably consistent the Bible is with the history of language!

The discovery that the writing of Adam's descendants was nonsyllabic is surprising, yet not surprising. A millennium of existence had taken place without a sophisticated common written language. A language with a few thousand characters may have been able to describe a complex situation, but it would have been tedious to read and write.[13] What is equally important is that it would have been difficult to use as a tool for thought.

Thought is best developed with a simplified writing system. If a student is doing poorly in school, he or she needs to do *more writing*! Writing helps recall and organization of thought. Many do not write their personal history because they remember nothing important to tell. Because of the way our brain is organized, processing input as a composite of present and past sensory impressions including words, many important memories are recalled only as we begin writing a first draft.

The Urim and Thummim is a communication of concept aid between sacred authors and sacred translators. Without that communication, translation of the *Book of Mormon* at first would have been almost impossible. If Joseph Smith memorized all of the characters used in First Nephi, it is unlikely that he could have properly translated Second Nephi without the Urim and Thummim. Chiasmatic passages, for example, would have certainly been less elegant.

The manner in which God operates through his children, as in the case of written language, shows his concern for upholding the principles of faith and free agency. This is the most exciting and rewarding part of his plan for us.

Neophyte Creators

"Why am I here and where am I going?" The answer is derived from God's statement "Man is that he might have joy." Our joy comes in discovery and achievement and also in the discoveries and achievements of our children. Without children our potential for joy is substantially reduced.

---

[13] This handicap was offset when God allowed Adam and his generation to live nearly 1,000 years.

Teachers may virtually teach the same concepts each year, but enjoy doing so as they see the enlightenment that comes into the lives of their students. If God receives joy from the accomplishments of his children, would we have been put on hold during the creation? If you were God, would you have waited until after the creation of the world and its creatures before creating man? If one believes that he lives and makes progress after death, why not before birth? A spirit living then should have learned about the creation. Creation is near the top of our list of our desired achievements.

With our imperfect knowledge, how could we create except by careful modification of a set of chromosomes in an existing organism? Evolution is not only God's way to preserve the important principle of living by faith, but is probably the only way we could have done it.

Some may say, "But I'm no scientist. How could I ever do such a thing?" One must remember that we are in the final quarter of the senior year of the University of the Universe and know a great deal more that we know here. But, even if we were slow in some subjects, we certainly could participate in a council of neophyte creators under the direction of Christ and Adam according to our ability and desire. A person with outstanding artistic ability could collaborate with a genetics expert in the creation of a beautiful new species of flower. But the God of God's and Lord of Lord's must know everything.

There are some who may never desire to do more than serve in such a council, just as there are many who may feel comfortable as an executive but would not want to have the responsibilities of the President of the United States. There are also some in the Church, for example, who reject the concept of polygamy because it seems to hard to live. (I mention polygamy in this book because no one ever talks about it, as if we want to forget it ever existed or will exist again.) Are we glad this principle has been taken away so we can act less responsibly, as did the children of Israel?[14] Would polygamy help solve the growing welfare problem that burdens our country because there is no father and breadwinner in many homes? Tens of billions of our tax dollars are spent each year to provide assistance to families with no father (which are allowed live-in boy friends). But the welfare problem is not as great as broken roles in broken homes.

---

[14] Deuteronomy 5:24-27.

If a married man was a good provider and married a widow or woman raising children without a husband, would not God smile upon and bless that man for his concern, if it was lawful for him to do so? Because of the welfare situation just mentioned it seems logical that polygamy will return to our country and then to the Church. Polygamy will apparently be practiced prior to the Millennium. During the wars[15] that precede it perhaps many men will die and *seven women shall take hold of one man, saying, We will eat our own bread, and wear our own apparel: only let us be called by thy name, to take away our reproach.* (Isaiah 4:1)

Celestial Families

We will only have a 'family' in the celestial kingdom on a volunteer basis. All will have the agency to choose to live with us or in some other dominion, just as when we chose to be with Christ rather than Lucifer. We must have something advantageous to offer. We must have love, charity, knowledge, wisdom, be in harmony with God and offer assistance in developing character, knowledge and virtue.

It is important that every one of God's children be "sealed" to someone who is standing on higher ground who will be responsible to fellowship them in the fullness of the gospel of Jesus Christ or supervise their pursuit of Eternal progression. God will not allow any of his children to be forgotten or left without hope. This is the purpose of the Family History program of the Church and the reason sealings are so important. Being sealed to someone carries a great deal of responsibility for that person. It is not just a matter of who you will live with in heaven. If we do not take our sealings responsibilities seriously, they will be given to someone else regardless of our earthly genealogies. We need to be sealed to someone standing on higher ground as well as to some standing on lower ground. Celestial beings will minister to Terrestrial beings, and Terrestrial beings will minister to Telestial beings (D & C 76:87,88).

The Lord admonished us in the last two verses of Section 121 of the *Doctrine and Covenants,*

---

[15] The destruction of the world by fire, the redness of the moon, the baldness of women (Isaiah 3:24) and hiding in caves of the earth (Isaiah 2:19) seem to indicate nuclear war.

> Let your bowels also be filled with charity towards all men, and to the household of faith, and let virtue garnish thy thoughts unceasingly; then shall thy confidence wax strong in the presence of God; and the doctrine of the priesthood shall distill upon thy soul as the dews from heaven. The Holy Ghost shall be thy constant companion, and thy scepter an unchanging scepter of righteousness and truth; and thy dominion shall be an everlasting dominion, and without compulsory means it shall flow unto thee forever and ever.

These two verses are so profound and beautiful they could only been written by revelation from God. No single person or committee could have produced them—or even the Sacramental prayers.[16] If a person needs another witness that God exists, he or she only has to ponder these declarations or take pen in hand and try to write something comparable.

I once asked, "How could the world have been made better than it now is?" Now I ask, "How would you have dealt with your children during the creation of the world if you were God?"

---

[16] D & C 20:77.

EPILOGUE

Pondering the truthfulness of what you read is always a challenge. It is difficult to be nonprejudiced. Those who have made up their mind before examining the evidence are prejudiced. Prejudice is a security blanket that avoids truth. One is not likely prejudiced against only one thing, since prejudice is a state of mind. Being non-prejudiced means being open-minded with all the patient research, prayer, testing theories, and tentative conclusions that it requires.

If the Bible was as it was originally penned, would it be literally-correct? Was Eve's body actually made from Adams rib? Joseph Smith states that everyone has a mother and a father. I believe that God, to show a symbolic one-ness and protective relationship that should exist between man and wife, did use one of Adam's ribs as *part* of the earthly elements to reconstruct Eve's body. Was the story of creation denied Adam's generation? If they were told the story of Eve's creation, would not Adam be constrained to demonstrate a missing rib? After reading the chapter on *Relativity and Resurrection,* another mystery is, perhaps, less mysterious.

It would be difficult for a General Authority to have written a book such as this. Not because of the material, but because of the interpretations of the readers. Even if the General Authority stated on each page that "this is my opinion." he would still be concerned that members would accept it as official doctrine. Besides, there are enough true experiences to relate without theorizing.

When giving instructions about the building of the Kirtland temple, the Lord said that it should be speedily built as a place of thanksgiving and instruction and "That they may be perfected in the understanding of their ministry, in theory, in principle, and in doctrine, in all things pertaining to the kingdom of God on the earth." (D & C 97:14) The only way a theory can be perfected is by testing it—by its fruits. If

God gives us all the answers, we will ever be dependent and our progression will come to a stop.

Where and how should theories be discussed? In church settings they should never be more than a brief aside to a lesson in an approved course of study. Theories are best reserved for books and independent study, in order to give an investigator ample time and background information.

The way we arrive at correct concepts is by study, testing theories, and revelation. Modern revelations in the *Book of Mormon* or the *Doctrine and Covenants* say very little about the creation. Perhaps God expects us to use the evidence at hand, as in D & C 88:79.

Because we learn precept upon precept, teachers occasionally may have unrefined opinions that are incorrect. Church members may become disaffected because of misinterpretations or misunderstandings which are opinion but are assumed to be doctrine. This is one reason why the courses of study in the church are the standard works. Would one want it otherwise? Would a book of catechisms, having all the answers where no thinking was necessary, be a better course?

One reason that evolution is so appealing is that the origin of the first intelligent life (God) needs some kind of explanation. After bypassing the unanswerable question "Why does anything exist" one finds elementary particles organized in a surprisingly complex manner which allow for solar systems, replicating structures and improbable, but possible, spontaneous evolution.

The evolutionary scenario, however, has two difficult aspects:

1. The creation of the first cell.
2. The orderly evolution of complex life.

Let us suppose that on a planet somewhere in the past, complex life, including man, did evolve by random evolution. (Although evolutionists talk of random evolution, what they see is not random but well ordered.[1]) The appearance of man would be difficult to randomly achieve, but let us assume that it did happen.

It may have been that man on our hypothetical planet may have lived a long time. Aging is a natural, universal property of all our living

---

[1] In *The Origin of Mutants, Nature,* September 1988, John Cairns et. al. state, "The main purpose of this paper is to show how insecure is our belief in the spontaneity (randomness) of most mutations. It seems to be a doctrine that has never been properly put to the test."

macroorganisms, but just as single cell organisms can live indefinitely, it is possible that a world of indefinitely living macroorganisms could have been created, including man. If such was not the case, let us suppose that someone eventually discovered how to prevent aging.

We know very little about other dimensions, but let us suppose that they exist and that the most intelligent being in such a world could incorporate corresponding indestructible dimensions to his body so that he was in no danger of being accidently killed. Thus would begin the world of spirits. It would be then evident that in order to prevent the accidental death of one's children, it would be better to create first a spiritual body.

In the previous scenario evolutionists must ask themselves if the god who could do these things would place his children on planets with orderly controlled evolution? Would he just wait and see what develops? What would you do, realizing that random evolution may not occur, would be very slow, or may not produce the plants and animals that would properly prepare the planet for your children? Why do evolutionists have resistance to the idea that such a god and controlled evolution exists when it has to be the end product of their own evolutionary scenarios?

Although evolutionists may not be able to see things in reverse order, LDS doctrine indicates that the spiritual creation and intelligences came first.

> *God himself, finding he was in the midst of spirits and glory* [other spirits were seeking his guidance and promising their obedience] *because he was more intelligent, saw proper to institute laws whereby the rest could have a privilege to advance like himself* (H.C. Vol. 6 p. 312.).
>
> *God saw that those intelligences had not power to defend themselves against those that had a tabernacle, therefore the Lord called them together in counsel and agreed to form them tabernacles... (The Words of Joseph Smith, p. 68).*

Creationists must also ask themselves if God would place his children on a planet with orderly controlled evolution, giving his children an opportunity for creative experiences. Creationists should welcome this idea when it is also one end product of their own eternal progression scenario to become like God.

The author welcomes any comments. One of the joys in my life is to refine my knowledge of truth—perhaps including such in a second edition.

>William E. Harris
>1235 Mission Road
>Salt Lake City, Utah 84104

INDEX

A

Abraham—15, 49, 75, 91
Adam—15, 34, 51, 75
Adam's rib—68, 145
Adam-God theory—75, 90
Adamic language—56, 134, 136
Age of solar system—20
Age of the Earth—15
Akkad—54, 136, 138
Angels—102-103
Animals on other worlds—102
Anthropomorphism—40
Apostates—127
Athanasian Creed—86
Athanasius—86
Atonement scriptures—122

B

Big bang—64
Biological survival—79
Bird migration—70
Blessings—120
Bloom's taxonomy—74
Bohr, Niels—13
Bruno, Giordano—87

C

Catastrophism—41
Celestial travel—111, 116
Champollion—137
Chaotic matter—18
Confusion of tongues—138

Continents—62, 68
Copernicus, Nicolaus—85
Covenants—102
Creation of a solar system—80
Creative experiences—34, 142
Cuneiform—48, 135

D

Dalton, John—20
Darkness—58, 60
Darwin, Charles—26
Davies, Paul—64, 99, 125
Day of creation—14
Disorganized globes—18
Dividing the Earth—136
Dust of the Earth—112

E

Earliest writing—135
Earth, a living soul—101
Earth-like planets—65, 67
Eber/Ebrium—49-50
Ebla—49-56
Einstein—13, 17, 86, 105-106, 109, 128
Elders in Ebla—53
Elements of the Earth—18-19
Entropy—60
Evil spirits—97-98
Evolution in Aplysia—71-72
Evolution in history—89
Evolutionary jumps—30, 35
Ex-Nihilo creation—20

F

Firmament—61
First cause—12
First flesh on Earth—34
Forces—128
Fortunate accidents—63, 64, 69

G

Gaia hypothesis—101
Galaxies—19
Galileo—85
Genetic engineering—34-35, 44, 103
Genetic defects—27, 32-33
Genetic exchange—45
Genetic corrections—27
Genetic programming—27
Genetically controlled behavior—71
Genomes—76
Glory—130-133
Gould, Stephen—30-31
Grace—126

H

Hawking, Steven—12
Hebrew—52
Hell—97, 121
Homosexuals—8182, 98
Human sexuality—80
Human instincts—79

I

Improbability of the Universe—64
Inquisition—87
Inspiration—119
Insulin—24

J

Jared—138
Johnson, Donald—29

Joy of discovery—134, 141
Judgement—123
Justice—126

K

Kepler, Johannes—85
Kolob—14, 17, 19, 132

L

Lavoisier, Antoine—21
Light—58
Light of Christ—128
Living solar systems—20
Longevity of man—32-33

M

Man as a creator—75, 83, 134, 141
Matthiae, Paulo—48, 52
Mercy—126
Milky Way galaxy—19
Missing links—35-36
Montague, Ashley—106
Moon—54, 63
Moses—68
Most High God—138
Mountain of the Lord's House—139
Multiple earths—65
Mutations—27-29, 45
Mysteries—117

N

Newton, Isaac—94-95
Nimrod—138-139

O

Origen—97

P

Parallel worlds—124
Pettinato, Giovanni—48, 51-52

Phelps, W. W.—15
Pictographic writing—135
Plato—95
Polygamy—90, 142
Power of resurrection—116
Prayer—104-105
Pre-Adamic hominids—35-37
Pre-existent programming—78
Principle of Ignorance—12

R

Raphael—104
Reasoning of prophets—91
Reasons for existence—72, 134
Redemption—126
Relativity—17, 109-110
Repentance—81-82, 123, 126
Resurrection—111-116
Revelation—104, 118
Roberts, B. H.—8
Role playing—80, 142
Rosetta Stone—137

S

Sacred history—137
Salvation in other worlds—124, 126
Sex offenders—8182
Shem—56, 135
Short cut to heaven—121
Smith, Joseph—18-19, 91-92
Smith, Joseph Fielding—8
Socrates—94-95
Sodom and Gomorrah—48
Solar systems—124
Space and time—16-17
Special creation—33, 41-45
Speciation & evolution—23-24
Spirit children—116
Spirit matter—99
Spirit of the Earth—101

Spiritual senses—129
Spiritual creation—78, 116
Spiritually controlled behavior—78
Spontaneous beginnings—59
Stars—19-20
Sumerians—55, 88, 135, 138
Supernovas—20
Syllabic writing—136, 138

T

Telestial influence—97
Terrestrial beings—125
Time—16
Tower of Babel—136, 138
Traditions—13, 121
Translation—125
Tree of life—32, 99
Trinity—86
Truth—105-107

U

Ultimate set of wheels—116
Uncertainty principle—13
Undetectable dimensions—99
Unification theories—100
Urey and Miller—67
Urim and Thummim—132, 140

V

Verbal warning—130
Vestigial organs—42